basic
ITALIAN
grammar

D1434435

PEMBANAGH COLLEGE
LIBRARY
CANCELLED 31 JUL 2023

RECEIVED 15 OCT 2002

basic
ITALIAN
grammar

Tony Giovanazzi

CANCELLED 3 1 JUL 2023

JOHN MURRAY

Other titles in this series
Basic French Grammar by Valerie Worth-Stylianou 0 7195 7121 9
Basic German Grammar by John Clapham 0 7195 7122 7
Basic Spanish Grammar by Richard Leathes 0 7195 7120 0

© Tony Giovanazzi 1996
First published 1996
by John Murray (Publishers) Ltd
50 Albemarle Street
London W1X 4BD

Copyright and copying
All rights reserved. This publication is copyright and may not be copied
except within the terms of a photocopying licence issued by the Copyright
Licensing Agency or by specific permission of the publisher.

Layouts by D&J Hunter
Typeset by Florencetype Ltd, Stoodleigh, Devon
Typeset in 11/12pt Galliard and 9/12 Frutiger
Printed and bound in Great Britain by the University Press, Cambridge

A CIP record for this book is available from the British Library.

ISBN 0 7195 8501 5

▼▼▼ CONTENTS

Introduction	vii
Spelling and pronunciation in Italian	1
Articles and nouns: identifying people, places and things	9
Adjectives: describing people, places and things	23
Adverbs: describing where, when and how something is done	45
Pronouns: replacements for nouns	54
Prepositions: describing how things relate to each other	72
Verbs: identifying what is happening	82
Doubts and commands: subjunctives and imperatives	122
Numbers	139
Dates and time	143
Verb tables	147
Answers to activities	155
Index	165

▼▼▼
INTRODUCTION

The aim of this book is to make the main points of Italian grammar accessible and memorable for anyone wishing to learn or revise them. It takes a very straightforward approach and does not assume that you are already familiar with grammatical terms.

- The purpose of each rule and structure is clearly explained.
- Examples taken from everyday language show how each point is applied and help you to remember the way it works.
- Activities give opportunities to practise or revise each point; answers to the activities are provided.

Basic Italian Grammar is suitable for independent revision or study, or for use alongside other course materials for reference and practice. It will be of invaluable help if you are in any of the following learning situations:

- working towards a language qualification or examination;
- taking a language component as part of a broader course such as business studies;
- brushing up your Italian in preparation for a holiday or business trip to an Italian-speaking country;
- improving your grasp of Italian for use at work.

▼▼▼
SPELLING AND PRONUNCIATION IN ITALIAN

Italian is pronounced as it is written. The few basic rules of spelling are really there to show how words are pronounced.

▼ Stress

Like English words, Italian words are pronounced with greater emphasis on one syllable than on the others. This is known as the 'stress' of the word. Most Italian words have the stress on the second-last syllable:

finestra = *window*, balcone = *balcony*

Some words have the stress on the last syllable. Where these end in a vowel, the stress is marked by an accent over the vowel:

città = *city*, più = *more*

A word that ends in a consonant is almost always a shortened form of a verb and has the stress in the same place as the full form:

cantar (cantare) = *to sing*, aver (avere) = *to have*

However, many Italian words have the stress on other syllables, and there is no way of telling from looking at them. This happens with English words as well. Think of 'entrance' (a way in) and 'entrance' (to charm). The only way to know how to pronounce a word with the stress in the right place is to learn the stress as you go along. To help you, in this book, where words do not have the stress on the second-last syllable, the syllable where the stress falls is underlined. For example:

prezzemolo = *parsley*   uomini = *men*
origano = *oregano*   dicendolo = *saying it*
maschera = *mask*   pagina = *page*

▼ *Written accents*

The only written accent used now by Italians is the grave accent (**à, è, ò**). It is written over a vowel:

- to mark the stress when the stress is at the end of the word (see page 1)

- in words of one syllable to clarify the meaning:
  è (= 'is') to distinguish it from **e** (= 'and')
  là (= 'there') to distinguish it from **la** (= 'the')
  sì (= 'yes') to distinguish it from **si** (= 'oneself')

You will sometimes see the acute accent (**é**) in print in the word **perché** (= 'why') to distinguish it from the word **perchè** (= 'because'), and also in the words **né** (= 'neither') to distinguish it from **ne** (= 'some of it'), and **sé** (= 'oneself') to distinguish it from **se** (= 'if'). It is not normal, though, in handwriting or typescript.

▼ The vowels

▼ *Hard vowels*

'A', 'o' and 'u' are known as 'hard vowels' because when they come after the letters 'c' or 'g' they harden the sound to 'k' (like the 'c' in 'cat') and 'g' (like the 'g' in 'got').

'a'

'**a**' is pronounced as in 'bad':

mamma = *mother*

'u'

'**u**' is pronounced as in 'through' (always the full open 'oo' sound):

luna = *moon*

'o'

'**o**' can be either a closed sound, as in 'boat' or 'wrote':

sono = *I am*
voce = *voice*

or an open sound as in 'bomb' or 'hot':

trova = *finds*
suoi = *his/hers*

There is no clear rule for this and it is safer for an English speaker to aim for the more open 'o' sound.

'ò' ('o' with a stress mark) is always the open sound.

▼ Soft vowels

'E' and 'i' are known as 'soft vowels', because when they come after the letters 'c' and 'g' they soften the sounds to 'ch' (as in 'chest') and 'j' (as in 'jest').

'e'

'e' can be either a closed sound as in 'maid' or 'hate':

francese = *French*
faceva = *was making*

or an open sound as in 'bed':

perla = *pearl*
prendo = *I take*

but there is no rule for this, since it depends on individuals and the part of Italy they come from. The usual 'accepted' pronunciation is somewhere between the closed and the open.

Note: 'e' at the end of a word is always pronounced.

'i'

'i' when it is stressed always has the 'ee' sound (as in 'sheep'):

mio, mia = *my*   io = *I*
farmacia = *pharmacy*   Lucia

When it is not stressed:

- Before another vowel, it sounds like the English 'y' at the beginning of a word (as in 'you'):

piede = *foot*
chiaro = *clear*
Antonio

- After 'c' or 'g' and before a hard vowel ('a', 'o', 'u'), it is not pronounced as such, but used as a sign telling us to pronounce the 'c' as a 'ch' (as in 'chin') and the 'g' as a 'j' sound (as in 'gin'):

ciabatta = *slipper*
bacio = *kiss*
acciughe = *anchovies*
fagiano = *pheasant*

giorno = *day*
giù = *down*
Luciano
Giovanni

Otherwise, two or more vowels coming together each keep their full sound:

- **'au'** as the 'ou' in 'out':

  lauro = *laurel, bayleaf*

- **'ai'** as the 'y' in 'my'

  mai = *never*

- **'oi'** as the 'oy' in 'boy':

  noi = *we*   corridoio = *corridor*

- **'ei'** an open 'e' (as in 'egg'), followed by 'ee' (as in 'feel'):

  lei = *she, you*   sei = *you are*

- **'uo'** almost as the 'wa' in 'wand', but with a more open 'o':

  uovo = *egg*   buono = *good*

▼ The consonants

What makes Italian look different from English are the combinations of letters with 'h' (**'ch'**, **'cch'**, **'gh'** and, very rarely, **'ggh'**). Just remember that the letter 'h' is used only as a sign telling us to pronounce the 'c' as a 'k' (as in 'cat') and the 'g' as a hard sound (as in 'got'). The only other use for 'h' is in parts of the verb **avere** (*'to have'*). It is never pronounced.

'**c**'

'**c**' before a soft vowel ('e', 'i') is pronounced 'ch' (as in 'chat'):

cento baci = *a hundred kisses*

but adding 'h' to it makes the 'k' sound (as in 'cat') (common in plural endings):

amiche = *female friends*   pochi = *few*

Before a hard vowel ('a', 'o', 'u'), 'c' is pronounced as 'k' ('cat'):

cantare = *to sing*   contare = *to count*

but adding 'i' to it makes the 'ch' sound ('chat'):

baciare = *to kiss*   cioccolato = *chocolate*

'*g*'

'**g**' follows the same pattern as 'c':

• Before a soft vowel, it is pronounced as 'j' (as in 'jet'):

gelato = *ice cream*   pagina = *page*

but adding 'h' to it makes the 'g' sound (as in 'get') (common in plural endings):

funghi = *mushrooms*   laghi = *lakes*

• Before a hard vowel, it is pronounced as 'g' ('get'):

gatto = *cat*   gonna = *skirt*

but adding 'i' to it makes the 'j' sound ('jet'):

fagioli = *beans*   ragione = *reason*

Note: the 'j' sound of the letter 'g' in Italian is like the English sound in 'gin' or 'jet'. It is not the softer 'zh' sound that is used in French.

'*sc*'

'**sc**' follows the same pattern:

• Before a soft vowel, it is pronounced as 'sh' in 'ship':

scena = *scene*   uscire = *to go out*

but adding 'h' to it makes the sound 'sk' as in 'sky':

scherzo = *joke*   maschera = *mask*

• Before a hard vowel, it is pronounced as 'sk':

scarpa = *shoe*   sconto = *discount*

but adding 'i' to it makes the sound 'sh':

sciarpa = *scarf*   asciutto = *dry*

'gn'

'gn' is pronounced like the 'ny' in 'canyon':

ognuno = *each one, everyone*   agnello = *lamb*

'gli'

'gli' is pronounced like 'lli' in 'million':

aglio = *garlic*   conchiglie = *shells*
degli = *of the*   tagliatelle

Note: 'gl' with other vowels is pronounced as in English:

inglese = *English*   gloria = *glory*

's'

's' has two sounds, the unvoiced and the voiced. An unvoiced sound is like a whisper, with only the breath sounding through the letter. A voiced sound is more like a hum, with the sound of the voice coming through the letter.

• The unvoiced 's' is like the 's' in 'hiss'. It is normally used at the beginning of a word:

soldi = *money*   sentire = *to hear*

or before an unvoiced consonant ('c', 'f', 'p', 'q', 't'):

scala = *stair*   vespa = *wasp*
pasqua = *Easter*   pasta
sforzo = *effort*

or after a consonant:

pensare = *to think*   salsiccia = *sausage*

• Double 'ss' is always the unvoiced sound:

passare = *to pass*

• The voiced 's' is like the 's' in 'as' or 'hose', or like the English 'z'. It is normally used before a voiced consonant ('b', 'd', 'g', 'l', 'm', 'n', 'r', 'v'):

sbocco = *way out*   sgabello = *stool*
slittare = *to slip*   snodare = *to untie*
sradicare = *to uproot*   asmatico = *asthmatic*
sdraio = *deckchair*   svedese = *Swedish*

- When 's' comes between two vowels, as in **casa** (= 'house'), it is usually pronounced as a voiced 's' ('z' sound) in the north of Italy but as an unvoiced 's' in the centre and south. It is best to learn from the people you are most in contact with.

'*z*'

'**z**' and '**zz**' are pronounced like either 'ts' or 'dz'. There is no clear rule and there is no difference between single and double 'z'. (However, it is never pronounced like the English 'z'.) For example, **mezzo** (= 'half') has the 'dz' sound, but **prezzo** (= 'price') has the 'ts' sound. You simply have to learn the pronunciation when you learn the word.

'*qu*'

'**qu**' is always pronounced like 'kw':

quattro = *four*   qui = *here*

'*gu*'

'**gu**' is always pronounced like 'gw':

guerra = *war*   guanto = *glove*

▼ *Double consonants*

These are always pronounced as double consonants. The best way to do this is to think of the first consonant as the end of one syllable and the second one as the beginning of the next syllable. In English, for example, when we say 'got to' we do not put a space between the two 't's, but we do not run them together to sound like a single 't', either. In the same way, in Italian, **otto** (= 'eight') is pronounced *ot-to*. In English, we pronounce two 'n' sounds in 'penknife', and the same double sound is used to pronounce **penna** in Italian.

It is often very important to pronounce the sound of the single consonant and that of the double consonant correctly, because the meaning of the word can change completely:

- **nono** means 'ninth', but **nonno** means 'grandad'
- **fato** means 'fate', but **fatto** means 'done'
- **pena** means 'pain', but **penna** means 'pen' (also 'feather')
- **sono** means 'I am', but **sonno** means 'sleep'.

▼ Activity 1   *Pronunciation*

The world is full of Italian menus, and customers (and sometimes waiters) cannot always pronounce the names of the dishes. You should be able to now. Try and pronounce the following, which often cause problems.

tagliatelle

bruschetta

origano

conchiglie

fettuccine

finocchi

radicchio

maraschino

orecchiette

maccheroni all'ammatriciana

gnocchi

pesce al sciroppo

pizza quattro stagioni

stracciatella

There are also lots of Italian names which English speakers usually get wrong. You can now get them right.

Don Giovanni (no 'i' sound in 'io')

Antonio (open 'o')

Genova

Brindisi

Nicola (man's name)

Lancia

la Gioconda

Cagliari

Medici

Guido ('gw')

Andrea (man's name)

Capri

There are also some tongue-twisters. Try these:

ghiaccio = *ice*

sciogliere = *to melt*

scegliere = *to choose*

chiacchierare = *to chatter*

▼▼▼
ARTICLES AND NOUNS
identifying people, places and things

▼ The indefinite article

In Italian, the word for 'a' (or 'an'), the **indefinite article**, takes the same gender as the noun it goes with.

▼ *Masculine*
- **un** before a consonant or a vowel:

un bambino = *a child (boy)*
un uomo = *a man*
un caffè = *a coffee*

- **uno** before 's' + consonant or 'z':

uno studio = *a study*
uno zio = *an uncle*

▼ *Feminine*
- **una** before a consonant (including 's' + consonant and 'z'):

una bambina = *a child (girl)*
una strada = *a street, a road*

- **un'** before a vowel:

un'automobile = *a car*
un'acqua minerale = *a mineral water*
un'aranciata = *an orangeade*
un'occasione = *a bargain, opportunity*

Note: only feminine nouns beginning with a vowel take **un'**. Masculine nouns beginning with a vowel take **un** without an apostrophe.

▼ *The number 'one'*

The indefinite article is also the word for the number 'one'. It always takes the gender of the noun it goes with. The context usually makes it clear if the meaning is the number 'one' or simply an indefinite 'a'.

Un caffè, un'aranciata e due cappuccini.	*One coffee, one orangeade and two cappuccinos.*
No ... prendo un caffè anch'io.	*No ... I'll have a coffee as well.*

The full form **uno/una** is always used when the article/ number is separated from its noun:

Due aranciate o una?	*Two orangeades or one?*
E due cappuccini. No, uno!	*And two cappuccinos. No, one!*

but when the number 'one' stands on its own or is used with the word **numero** it is always **uno**:

uno, due, tre = *one, two, three*
numero uno = *number one*

▼ The definite article ('the')

The **definite article** (the word for 'the') takes the same gender (masculine or feminine) and the same number (singular or plural) as the noun it goes with.

▼ *Masculine*

Singular	Plural	When used	Example
il	i	before a consonant (except 's' + consonant or 'z')	il vino, i vini = *the wine(s)*
l'	gli	before a vowel	l'occhio, gli occhi = *the eye(s)*
lo	gli	before 's' + consonant or 'z'	lo zaino, gli zaini = *the backpack(s)*

▼ *Feminine*

Singular	Plural	When used	Example
la	le	before any consonant	la donna, le donne = *the woman, women*
l'	le	before a vowel	l'oliva, le olive = *the olive(s)*

Note: **gli** and **le** are sometimes shortened to **gl'** and **l'** when they come before a noun beginning with a vowel, but this is becoming less common in modern Italian.

▼ Use of the article

It is important to know when to include or leave out the article in Italian.

* The indefinite article is usually left out when referring to someone's profession, nationality, rank or religion:

Roberto è **medico**.	*Roberto is a doctor.*
La signora è **americana**.	*The lady is (an) American.*
Suo marito è **capitano della Nazionale**.	*Her husband is captain of the national team.*
È **cattolica**.	*She is a Catholic.*

but the article is kept in when the noun is qualified in any way at all:

Roberto è **un medico eminente**.	*Roberto is an eminent doctor.*
La signora è **un'**americana sposata con un calciatore italiano.	*The lady is an American married to an Italian footballer.*

* The definite article is used in Italian when the noun has an abstract or general sense, unlike English, which drops the article.

Il silenzio è oro.	*Silence is golden.*
L'oro è caro.	*Gold is expensive.*
Le donne italiane sono eleganti.	*Italian women are elegant.*
Il latte è per **i** bambini.	*Milk is for babies.*

- The definite article is used when referring to people by their title:

| il signor Mancini | Mr Mancini |
| il dottor Bianchi | Dr Bianchi |

but it is not used when you are addressing them directly:

| Buongiorno, signor Mancini | Good morning, Mr Mancini |
| Caro dottor Bianchi | Dear Dr Bianchi (as in a letter) |

- The definite article is also used with the names of countries when these stand on their own:

L'Italia è bella.	Italy is beautiful.
La Francia è grande.	France is big.
Il Giappone è prospero.	Japan is prosperous.

but it is not used when the name has a word such as **in** or **di** in front of it:

| Le città **d'**Italia sono interessanti. | The cities of Italy are interesting. |
| **In** Francia si mangia bene. | People eat well in France. |

▼ Activity 1   *Put in the article*

Use appropriate articles to complete the following:

a   *a woman:* .... donna
b   *men:* .... uomini
c   *a student:* .... studente
d   *the house:* .... casa
e   *the chairs:* .... sedie
f   *one boy:* .... ragazzo
g   *an aerial:* .... antenna
h   *the children:* .... bambini
i   *the students:* .... studenti
j   *the purchases:* .... acquisti
k   *silver:* .... argento
l   *an egg:* .... uovo
m   *the uncle:* .... zio
n   *the boots:* .... stivali

Insert the correct article in the gap, where it is appropriate to use one.

o   Il signor Volante è .... professore.
p   È .... bravo professore.
q   La ragazza è .... americana.
r   È in .... camera numero uno.
s   .... americani sono simpatici.

▼ Masculine and feminine nouns

A noun is a word that names something: e.g. the **price** of **coffee**, a **game** of **football**.

Nouns in Italian are either masculine or feminine. The gender is usually clear from the ending, but not always. This means it is better to learn nouns along with their articles, (**il**, **la**, **lo**).

▼ *Nouns ending in '-o'*

Almost all nouns ending in '**-o**' are masculine. The ending changes to '**-i**' to form the plural:

il giorno, i giorni = *the day(s)*
l'albero, gli alberi = *the tree(s)*

Common exception

la mano (feminine) = *the hand*
le mani (feminine) = *the hands*

■ Feminine words ending in '-o'

Some nouns ending in '**-o**' are really shortened forms of longer feminine nouns, so are still feminine. They do not change in the plural:

la radio, le radio = *the radio(s)* (*originally* la radiotelegrafia)
la moto, le moto = *the motorbike(s)* (la motocicletta)
la foto, le foto = *the photo(s)* (la fotografia)

▼ Activity 2   *Masculine plurals*

Put into the plural:

a il giorno (= *the day*)
b il letto (= *the bed*)
c lo zucchino (= *the courgette*)
d l'angolo (= *the corner*)

e il conto (= *the bill*)
f lo sforzo (= *the effort*)
g il panino (= *the bread roll*)
h l'ingresso (= *the entrance*)

▼ *Nouns ending in -a*

Almost all nouns ending in '-**a**' are feminine. The ending changes to '-**e**' to form the plural:

la tavola, le tavole = *the table(s)*
la sedia, le sedie = *the chair(s)*
l'acqua, le acque = *the water(s)*

But:

A few nouns ending in '-**a**' are in fact masculine and form their plural with '-**i**':

il pilota, i piloti = *the pilot(s)*
il programma, i programmi = *the programme(s)*
il problema, i problemi = *the problem(s)*

Common exception

il cinema ('*the cinema*') does not change in the plural:
i cinema = *the cinemas*

▼ **Activity 3**   *Feminine plurals*

Put into the plural:

a la signora (= *the lady*)
b la tazza (= *the cup*)
c l'oliva (= *the olive*)
d la scarpa (= *the shoe*)
e la forchetta (= *the fork*)
f la saponetta (= *the bar of soap*)
g l'anatra (f.) (= *the duck*)
h l'aroma (m.) (= *the aroma*)

▼ *Nouns ending in -e*

Some nouns ending in '-**e**' are masculine, while others are feminine. The plural ending is always '-**i**':

il padre, i padri = *the father(s)*
la madre, le madri = *the mother(s)*
il piede, i piedi = *the foot, feet*
la voce, le voci = *the voice(s)*
l'automobile, le automobili (f.) = *the car(s)*
l'amore, gli amori (m.) = *love(s)*

■ **Nouns ending in '-ione'**

Nouns ending in '-**ione**' are always feminine. Since they end in -**e**, the plural ending is always -**i**:

la missione, le missioni = *the mission(s)*
la pressione, le pressioni = *the pressure(s)*
l'azione, le azioni = *the action(s)*
la nazione, le nazioni = *the nation(s)*

▼ **Activity 4** *Plurals of nouns ending in -e*

Put into the plural:

a la notte (= *the night*)
b il fiore (= *the flower*)
c la lente (= *the lens*)
d l'unione (= *the union*)
e la croce (= *the cross*)
f il colore (= *the colour*)
g il giocatore (= *the player*)
h l'orefice (= *the jeweller*)

▼ *Variable nouns*

Nouns that refer to people can be variable in gender:

• A noun ending in '-**ista**' may be masculine **or** feminine, depending on whether it refers to a male or a female. The masculine plural ending is '-**i**', the feminine plural ending is '-**e**'. The masculine plural form is used in a general sense when there is no specific reference to male or female:

l'artista   *the artist* (male or female)
gli artisti   *(the) artists* (artists in general, or male artists)
le artiste   *(the) female artists*

Other common examples are:

farmacista = *chemist*
giornalista = *journalist*
turista = *tourist*

Adjectives agree with the gender and number of the noun as usual:

il turista americano   *the American tourist* (a man)
la turista americana   *the American tourist* (a woman)
i turisti americani   *(the) American tourists* (in general or male)
le turiste americane   *(the) American tourists* (female)

- Certain nouns ending in '**-a**' or '**-e**' may be masculine **or** feminine, depending on whether they refer to a male or a female:

il collega, i colleghi   *the male colleague(s)*
('gh' for the 'g' sound)
la collega, le colleghe   *the female colleague(s)*
('gh' for the 'g' sound)
il nipote, i nipoti   *the nephew(s), grandson(s),*
     grandchildren
la nipote, le nipoti   *the niece(s), granddaughter(s)*
il cantante, i cantanti   *the (male) singer(s)*
la cantante, le cantanti   *the (female) singer(s)*

- Some nouns change their ending according to whether they are masculine or feminine:

'-o' to '-a'

il maestro, la maestra   *the teacher*
(plural: i maestri, le maestre)
il sarto, la sarta (plural: i sarti,   *the tailor/dressmaker*
le sarte)

'-e' to '-a'

il cameriere, la cameriera   *the waiter, waitress (or maid)*
(plural: i camerieri, le cameriere)
il signore, la signora   *the gentleman, lady*
(plural: i signori, le signore)
l'infermiere, l'infermiera (plural: *the nurse*
gli infermieri, le infermiere)

'-ore' to '-oressa'

il professore, la professoressa   *the teacher (also professor)*
(plural: i professori, le professoresse)

'*-tore*' to '*-trice*'

l'attore, l'attrice (plural: *the actor, actress*
gli attori, le attrici)
il direttore, la direttrice   *the director/manager, manageress*
(plural: i direttori, le direttrici)
l'autore, l'autrice (plural: *the author, authoress*
gli autori, le autrici)

Common exception

il dottore, la dottoressa   *the doctor*
(plural: i dottori, le dottoresse)

- A few nouns are feminine even if they refer to males:

la guardia, le guardie = *the guard(s)*
la guida, le guide = *the guide(s)*
la scorta, le scorte = *the escort(s)*
la sentinella, le sentinelle = *the sentry (sentries)*

▼ Making a noun plural

▼ *Unchanging plurals*
Some nouns do not change in the plural:

- nouns ending in a stressed vowel:

la città, le città = *the city, cities*
la virtù, le virtù = *the virtue(s)*
la difficoltà, le difficoltà = *the difficulty, difficulties*
un caffè, due caffè = *a (one) coffee, two coffees*
un tè, due tè = *a (one) tea, two teas*

- nouns of foreign origin ending in a consonant:

il gas, i gas = *the gas(es)*
lo sport, gli sport   *the sport(s)*
il foulard, i foulard = *the scarf, scarves*

- nouns ending in '**-i**' or '**-ie**':

la crisi, le crisi = *the crisis, crises*
una serie, due serie = *a (one) series, two series*

Common exception

La moglie (= the wife') becomes **le mogli** (= 'the wives').

• family names:

i Rossi = *the Rossis*
i Cocozza = *the Cocozzas*

▼ *Changes of form and gender*

Some nouns ending in '-o' are masculine in the singular, but for the plural the ending changes to '-a', and they also become feminine in gender:

il braccio, le braccia = *the arm(s)*
il dito, le dita = *the finger(s)*
il labbro, le labbra = *the lip(s)*
il ginocchio, le ginocchia = *the knee(s)*
il ciglio, le ciglia = *the eyelash(es)*
il lenzuolo, le lenzuola = *the bedsheet(s)*
il paio, le paia = *the pair(s)*
l'uovo, le uova = *the egg(s)*
il muro, le mura = *the wall(s)*

Many of these also have a regular masculine plural ending in '-i':

ginocchi   lenzuoli   muri

Note:
i diti (usually **i diti del piede**) means 'the toes', while **le dita** means 'the fingers'.

Sometimes a plural form ending with '-i' is used in expressions with a more figurative meaning:

i **cigli** di una fossa   *the edges of a ditch*
i **bracci** di un candelabro   *the arms of a candelabra*

▼ *Irregular plurals*

Some common nouns have an irregular plural form:

la mano, le mani = *the hand(s)*   l'ala, le ali = *the wing(s)*
la moglie, le mogli = *the wife, wives*   l'arma, le armi = *the weapon(s)*
l'uomo, gli uomini = *the man, men*   il dio, gli dei = *the god, gods*

▼ Spelling changes to keep the sound

Masculine nouns ending in '-**co**' change to '-**chi**' in the plural to keep the 'k' sound:

il sacco, i sacchi = *the sack(s)/bag(s)*
il cuoco, i cuochi = *the cook(s)*

But:

There are exceptions, especially with words of more than one syllable, where the ending changes to '-**ci**' and therefore the sound changes from 'k' to 'ch':

l'amico, gli amici = *the friend(s)*
il nemico, i nemici = *the enemy, enemies*
il medico, i medici = *the doctor(s)*
il meccanico, i meccanici = *the mechanic(s)*

Feminine nouns ending in '-**ca**' always change to '- **che**' in the plural, keeping the 'k' sound:

l'amica, le amiche = *the friend(s) (female)*
la nemica, le nemiche = *the enemy, enemies (female)*
la cuoca, le cuoche = *the cook(s) (female)*
la bistecca, le bistecche = *the steak(s)*

Nouns ending in '-**go**' or '-**ga**' change to '-**ghi**' or '-**ghe**' in the plural, keeping the 'g' sound (as in 'get'):

l'albergo, gli alberghi = *the hotel(s)*
il luogo, i luoghi = *the place(s)*
il catalogo, i cataloghi = *the catalogue(s)*
la bottega, le botteghe = *the shop(s)*
la collega, le colleghe = *the colleague(s) (female)*

Common exception

l'asparago, gli asparagi = *asparagus*

When a noun ending in '-**ga**' is masculine it changes to '-**ghi**' in the plural:

il collega, i colleghi = *the colleague(s)*

▼ *Nouns ending in -io*

Nouns ending in '-**io**' (where the 'i' is not stressed) change to '-**i**' in the plural:

l'occhio, gli occhi = *the eye(s)*
il negozio, i negozi = *the shop(s)*
il figlio, i figli = *the son(s)*
lo studio, gli studi = *the study, studies*

But:

There are a very few nouns ending in '**io**' where the stress falls on the 'i' of the ending, and for these the plural becomes '-**ii**':

lo zio, gli zii = *the uncle(s)*
l'addio, gli addii = *the farewell(s)*

▼ *Nouns ending in -ia*

- Where the 'i' of the ending is stressed, the plural ending simply changes from '-**a**' into '-**e**':

la farmacia, le farmacie = *the chemist's shop(s)*
la pasticceria, le pasticcerie = *the pastry shop(s)*
la trattoria, le trattorie = *the restaurant(s)*
la sinfonia, le sinfonie = *the symphony, symphonies*
la tecnologia, le tecnologie = *the technology, technologies*

- Where the 'i' of the ending is not stressed, it may stay in the spelling of the plural ending:

la camicia, le camicie = *the shirt(s)*
la valigia, le valigie = *the suitcase(s)*
la famiglia, le famiglie = *the family, families*

But:

In some words, the 'i' drops out:

la faccia, le facce = *the face(s)*
la spiaggia, le spiagge = *the beach(es)*

There is no hard and fast rule, and you may see both spellings of the ending used. It makes no difference to the pronunciation.

▼ Adding endings (suffixes) to nouns

It is extremely common in Italian to add an ending to nouns (and also to adjectives and adverbs) to give a different flavour to the meaning or even to change the meaning altogether. These suffixes may add the idea of smallness, largeness, endearment or nastiness. There are a number of different suffixes for each of these ideas, but they cannot all be tacked on to any word. The non-Italian can only keep eyes and ears open and stick to the ones which are most often used:

• The commonest suffixes are:

-ino, **-ina**, etc.
-etto, **-etta**, etc.
-ello, **-ella**, etc.

All of these mean 'little' and often mean 'dear little'. For example, **la mano** becomes **la manina** (plural: **le manine**). Children always have **manine**, never **mani**. Note that **mano** has a regular feminine form when it becomes **manina**.

il pane = *bread*	il panino = *the bread roll*
un bacio = *a kiss*	un bacino = *a little kiss* (but you may also hear **un bacetto**)
mio fratello = *my brother*	mio fratellino = *my little brother*
la casa = *the house*	la casetta = *the little house*
un vecchio = *an old man*	un vecchietto = *a little old man*
l'asino = *the donkey*	l'asinello = *the little donkey*

You have to be careful, since sometimes the meaning can be entirely different:

le manine = *the (sweet) little hands*   le manette = *the handcuffs*

Nouns which end in '**-one**' or '**-on**' add '**-cino**' rather than just '**-ino**':

un camion = *a truck, lorry*	un camioncino = *a little truck, a van*
un bottone = *a button*	un bottoncino = *a little button*

• The commonest suffix meaning 'big' is '**-one**', '**-ona**', etc.:

un fiasco = *a flask, bottle*   un fiascone = *a big flask, bottle*

Often, a feminine noun changes to masculine when you add the suffix '**-one**':

una bottiglia = *a bottle*   un bottiglione = *a big bottle*

- The commonest suffix meaning 'nasty' or 'unpleasant' is '**-accio**':

un lavoro = *work, a job*   un lavoraccio = *rotten work/job*

Thus you can have:

un ragazzo = *a boy*   un ragazzino/ragazzetto = *a little boy*
un ragazzone = *a big*   un ragazzaccio = *a lout*
(heavily built) boy

Suffixes are also very often added to names:

Gianni, Giannino; Antonia, Antonietta; Maria, Marietta, Mariolina (hence Lina); Giorgio, Giorgione

---

▼ Activity 5   *Articles and plurals*

Fill in the blanks, using first the appropriate indefinite article ('a/an'), and then the appropriate definite article ('the').

a	.... forno (= *oven*)	k	.... guanto (= *glove*)
b	.... fuoco (= *fire*)	l	.... fiamma (= *flame*)
c	.... cucina (= *kitchen*)	m	.... pentola (= *pot*)
d	.... bicchiere (m.) (= *glass*)	n	.... peperone (= *sweet pepper*)
e	.... luce (f.) (= *light*)	o	.... arancia (= *orange*)
f	.... sgabello (= *stool*)	p	.... straccio (= *rag, duster*)
g	.... erba (= *grass, herb*)	q	.... odore (m.) (= *odour, smell*)
h	.... gas (m.) (= *gas*)	r	.... manon (f.) (= *hand*)
i	.... dito (= *finger*)	s	.... uovo (= *egg*)
j	.... carne (f.) (= *meat*)	t	.... bistecca (= *steak*)

Now put each noun into the plural, using appropriate forms of the definite article.

ADJECTIVES
describing people, places and things

An adjective is a word that describes a noun:

Mio marito è **geloso.**   *My husband is jealous.*

▼ Making adjectives agree with the noun they describe

Each adjective must 'agree' in gender (masculine or feminine) and number (singular or plural) with the noun it describes. This agreement is shown in the ending of the word. For example, an adjective describing a feminine singular noun, such as **la giacca**, must also be in the feminine singular form.

una giacca **scura** = *a dark jacket*

The following table shows how the endings of adjectives change.

Masculine	piccolo	piccoli	(little, small)
Feminine	piccola	piccole	
Masc./fem.	grande	grandi	(big, great)
(adjectives	facile	facili	(easy)
ending in -e)	giovane	giovani	(young)

un piccolo sforzo (masc. sing.) = *a little effort*
spese piccole (fem. pl.) = *small expenses*

Note: adjectives ending in '**-e**' have only one form in the singular and one in the plural:

un lavoro facile (masc. sing.) = *an easy task*
grandi speranze (fem. pl.) = *great expectations*

The adjective must agree even when it is separated from the noun.

Le spese di mia moglie non sono piccole.   *My wife's expenses are not small.*

Where the adjective refers to two (or more) nouns it becomes plural and

- agrees with the nouns if they are both of the same gender
- becomes masculine plural if the nouns are of different genders.

La giacca e la gonna sono **scure** . . .
. . . ma vanno bene con una
camicia e un foulard **chiari**.

The jacket and the skirt are dark . . .
. . . but they go well with a light-
coloured shirt and scarf.

Note: some adjectives of colour never change, e.g. **rosa** (= 'pink'), **viola** (= 'purple'), **blu** (= 'blue'):

scarpe **rosa** = *pink shoes*
un vestito **viola** = *a purple dress*
i caschi **blu** = *the blue helmets* (name given to United Nations forces)

■ Irregular adjective endings

Adjectives ending in -co', '-ca' change to '-chi', '-che' in the plural (to keep the 'k' sound):

bianco, bianca, bianchi, bianche = *white*
poco, poca, pochi, poche = *little, few*

There are a few exceptions, where adjectives ending in '-co', '-ca' change to '-ci' in the masculine plural (changing the sound to the equivalent of English 'ch') but keep the feminine plural ending as '-che' (and the sound 'k'):

simpatico, simpatica, simpatici, simpatiche = *nice*
antipatico = *not nice*
magnifico = *magnificent*

Adjectives ending in '-go', '-ga' change to '-ghi', '-ghe' in the plural (to keep the hard 'g' sound):

lungo, lunga, lunghi, lunghe = *long*

Adjectives ending in '-io' (where the 'i' is not stressed) change to '-i' in the plural:

vecchio, vecchi = *old*   vario, vari = *various*

Adjectives ending in 'io' where the 'i' is stressed are very uncommon.

▼ Activity 1   *Making adjectives agree*

Put each adjective in brackets (the masculine singular form) in the correct form to agree with the noun.

a La Casa (bianco).
b Il mondo è (piccolo).
c La cravatta è (rosso) e (nero).
d I miei genitori sono (vecchio).
e Le ragazze sono (giovane).
f La strada non è (difficile), ma è (lungo).

▼ Position of adjectives

Adjectives usually come after the noun:

una camera doppia in un albergo   *a double room in a quiet hotel*
tranquillo

However, whether they come in front of or after the noun is often a matter of personal choice rather than strict rule. As a general guide, adjectives come after the noun when the literal meaning is being emphasised or a distinction is being underlined, and in front when a vaguer, more figurative sense is intended:

una povera donna = *a poor woman* (unfortunate)
una donna povera = *a poor woman* (who has no money)
un piccolo albergo = *a small hotel* (unpretentious)
un albergo piccolo = *a small hotel* (actually small)
la vecchia città = *the old town*
la città vecchia = *the ancient part of the town*
una bella ragazza = *a pretty girl* (the usual nice thing to say)
una ragazza bella = *a pretty girl* (emphasising that she really is pretty)

Sometimes the change in emphasis gives a different slant to the meaning:

una macchina nuova = *a new car* (brand new)
una nuova macchina = *a new car* (which may or may not be brand new)
un amico vecchio = *an old friend* (who is actually old)
un vecchio amico = *a friend of long standing*

Sometimes the position of the adjective changes its meaning completely:

numerose famiglie = *many families*
famiglie numerose = *large families*
diversi articoli = *several articles*
articoli diversi = *different articles, a variety of articles*

Adjectives describing colour or nationality always come after the noun:

una ragazza **inglese** dai capelli **biondi**   *an English girl with fair hair*

▼ Shortening of adjectives

Buono (= 'good') and **grande** (= 'big', 'great') follow the pattern of **un/uno** in front of masculine singular nouns:

- **buon** before a masculine singular noun (whether it begins with a vowel or a consonant, except for 's' + consonant):

un **buon** film = *a good film*
un **buon** affare = *a good (piece of) business, a good deal*

- **buono** before a masculine singular noun beginning with 's' + consonant:

un **buono** scrittore = *a good writer*

- either **buon** or **buono** before other nouns which require **uno**:

un **buon** (buono) zio = *a good uncle*
un **buon** (buono) psicologo = *a good psychologist*

- **gran** before a masculine singular noun beginning with a consonant:

un **gran** tenore = *a great tenor*

but one may use the full form as well:

È un anello di **grande** valore sentimentale.   *It's a ring of great sentimental value.*

- **grande** before a masculine singular noun beginning with a vowel or with 's' + consonant:

il **grande** amore di Giulietta e Romeo   *the great love of Romeo and Juliet*

un **grande** stabilimento = *a large factory*
un **grande** sforzo = *a great effort*

Note: **grande** also shortens to **gran** in the feminine singular when it comes before another adjective and has the meaning of 'very':

Sofia Loren è una **gran bella** donna. *Sofia Loren is a very beautiful woman.*

■ Big/great
Grande can mean both 'big' (size) and 'great' (quality or importance). The context usually makes it clear which meaning is intended, but often **grande** is used after the noun to emphasise the meaning of 'big'.

Un ristorante **grande** non è sempre un **gran** ristorante ... dipende dalla cucina. A big restaurant is not always a great restaurant ... it depends on the cooking.

Bello (= 'beautiful') has endings like those of the definite article ('the') when it comes **before** the noun:

• **bel** before a masculine singular noun beginning with a consonant:

un **bel** quadro = *a lovely picture*
un **bel** dì* = *one fine day*
* the famous aria from *Madame Butterfly*

• **bell'** before a masculine singular noun beginning with a vowel:

un **bell'**amore = *a beautiful love*

• **bello** before a masculine singular noun beginning with 's' + consonant or 'z':

un **bello** scherzo! = *a fine joke! some trick!*

• **bei** before a masculine plural noun beginning with a consonant:

i **bei** fiori = *the lovely flowers*

• **begli** before a masculine plural noun beginning with a vowel, 's' + consonant or 'z':

Che **begli** occhi!	*What beautiful eyes!*
Guardate i **begli** spaghetti!	*Look at the lovely spaghetti!*

Bello and **belli** are used only when they come after the noun or on their own:

Bei guanti! Sì, sono **belli**.	*Lovely gloves! Yes, they're lovely.*

(See also **quello**, page 36.)

The feminine forms **buona (buon')**, **buone**, **bella (bell')**, **belle** and **grande**, **grandi** follow the normal pattern.

■ Note on 'santo'

Santo as an adjective meaning 'holy' follows a normal pattern:

il Santo Padre = *the Holy Father*
il Santo Vangelo = *the Holy Gospel*

Santo as a title meaning 'saint' (masculine) shortens to **San**:

San Giovanni = *St John*

but not before names beginning with a vowel or 's' + consonant:

Sant'Antonio = *St Anthony*
Santo Stefano = *St Stephen*

▼ Adding endings (suffixes) to adjectives

(See also page 21.)

The suffixes '**-ino**', '**-one**' etc. are often used with adjectives:

È **carina** questa bambina.	*This child is sweet.*
Giorgio è **simpaticone**.	*Giorgio is a nice big fellow.*
Il vestito rosso è **grandino**.	*The red dress is a bit big.*

Note: when a suffix is added to an adjective, the stress moves to the second-last syllable, so **simpatico** becomes **simpaticone**.

▼ **Activity 2**   *Putting the adjective in the right place*

Choosing the most appropriate form and position, use the adjectives in brackets to complete the following sentences. You may also need to change the form of the article.

a   <u>La ragazza</u> è innamorata (<u>po</u>vera).
b   Roberto è <u>un compagno di classe</u> (vecchio).
c   Che <u>fiori</u> (belli)!
d   Questo è <u>un esempio</u> del lavoro di <u>uno scultore</u> (buono, grande).

▼ More or less: comparing adjectives

In English, we have three ways of comparing things:

- We change the ending of the adjective, as in 'big', 'bigger', 'the biggest'.

- We use 'more' and 'the most' or 'less' and 'the least' in front of the adjective.

- In a few cases, we change the word completely, as in 'good', 'better', 'the best'.

Italian has no equivalent of the '-er', (comparative) and '-est' (superlative) endings. It uses:

- **più** (comparative) and **il più** (superlative) for 'more' and 'the most' (changing **il** to **la**, **i**, or **le** to agree with the noun);

- **meno** (comparative) and **il meno** (superlative) for 'less' and 'the least' (again changing **il** to agree with the noun).

La casa della nonna è **meno grande** ma **più comoda**.	*Grandma's house is less big but more comfortable.*
La borsetta nera è **la meno cara** ma **la più bella**.	*The black handbag is the least expensive but the nicest.*

Note: **meno** and **più** do not change their form to agree with nouns.

▼ *Positioning 'più' and 'meno'*

Adjectives with **più** can go before or after the noun:

la **più bella** ragazza del mondo
la ragazza **più bella** del mondo } *the most beautiful girl in the world*

Note: when it comes after the noun, the article for the superlative (**il**, **la**, etc.) is not repeated. It is usually clear from the context whether the comparative 'more' or the superlative 'most' is meant. However, when the comparative is not accompanied by other words (such as **del mondo**, as in the above example), then it is better to put it after the noun:

Preferisco il vestito **più lungo**.   *I prefer the longer dress.*

Adjectives with **meno** always go after the noun:

la vacanza **meno piacevole** della mia vita   *the least pleasant holiday of my life*
Adottiamo la soluzione **meno cara**.   *Let's adopt the less/least expensive solution.*

▼ *The absolute superlative: '-issimo'*

Adding the ending '**-issimo**' (and '**-issima**', '**-issimi**', '**-issime**') to the stem of the adjective gives the meaning 'very', whereas **il più** means 'the most' (of a series):

Sì, la borsetta nera è **bellissima**, però non è **la più bella**.   *Yes, the black handbag is very beautiful, but it's not the nicest.*

Because it can stand alone, '**-issimo**' is called the **absolute superlative**, while **il più**, as one of a series, is called the **relative superlative**.

▼ *Irregular comparative and superlative forms*

A few very common adjectives change their form completely for comparative and superlative, but note that all of these can also be used in the normal pattern.

Adjective	Comparative	Relative superlative	Absolute superlative
buono	migliore	il migliore	ottimo
	più buono	il più buono	buonissimo
good	*better*	*the best*	*very good, excellent*

cattivo	peggiore	il peggiore	pessimo
	(più cattivo)	(il più cattivo)	(cattivissimo)
bad	*worse*	*the worst*	*very bad, dreadful*
grande	maggiore	il maggiore	massimo
	(più grande)	(il più grande)	(grandissimo)
big	*bigger*	*the biggest*	*very big, maximum*
piccolo	minore	il minore	minimo
	(più piccolo)	(il più piccolo)	(piccolissimo)
small	*smaller*	*the smallest*	*very small, minimum*

Note: when 'the greatest' and 'the least' describe an abstract noun, rather than the physical size of something, the forms **il massimo** and **il minimo** are used:

con **minimo** disturbo = *with very little trouble*
con **il minimo** disturbo = *with the least (i.e. the minimum) trouble*
con **massimo** rispetto = *with very great respect*
con **il massimo** rispetto = *with the greatest (i.e. the maximum) respect*

▼ *More than, less than*
- Use **più di** for 'more than' and **meno di** for 'less than' in expressions of quantity involving figures:

Quell'uomo pesa **più di** cento chili.	*That man weighs more than 100 kilos.*
Ho pagato **meno di** ventimila lire.	*I paid less than 20,000 lire.*

- Use **più . . . di** and **meno . . . di** when comparing two (or more) nouns or pronouns that stand alone:

Milano è **più** grande **di** Firenze.	*Milan is bigger than Florence.*
Mia mamma è **meno** alta **di** me.	*My mother is not as tall as me.*

- Use **più . . . che** and **meno . . . che** when there are phrases involved rather than single nouns or pronouns:

Fa **più** freddo in Inghilterra **che** in Italia.	*It is colder in England than in Italy.*
È **più** comodo prendere l'aereo **che** fare il viaggio in macchina.	*It's more comfortable to take the plane than to make the journey by car.*

- Use **più** . . . **che** and **meno** . . . **che** when two adjectives are being compared (the equivalent of the English 'rather than'):

Mio marito è **più** robusto **che** grasso. — *My husband is more well-built than fat (well-built rather than fat).*

Il vestito è **più** rosa **che** rosso. — *The dress is more pink than red.*

▼ '*As* . . . *as*'

There are several different ways to say 'as . . . as':

- The simplest way is to use **come** (= 'as, like'):

Domingo è bravo **come** Pavarotti. — *Domingo is as good as Pavarotti.*

- You can also use **così** . . . **come**, especially in the negative:

Domingo è **così** popolare **come** Pavarotti. — *Domingo is as popular as Pavarotti.*

Firenze **non è così** grande **come** Milano. — *Florence is not as big as Milan.*

- Alternatively, you can use **(tanto)** . . . **quanto**:

Domingo è **(tanto)** famoso **quanto** Pavarotti. — *Domingo is as famous as Pavarotti.*

Tanto and **quanto** do not change to agree with the noun:

La tua cravatta è **(tanto)** bella **quanto** la sua. — *Your tie is just as nice as his.*

Note: **tanto** on its own also means 'so' (in the sense of 'very'):

L'aria è **tanto** fresca. — *The air is so cool.*

▼ Activity 3   *Making comparisons*

Translate the words in brackets, using appropriate forms in suitable positions.

a Dov'è la fermata (nearest)?
b L'arrosto è (excellent), e (so) saporito, ma il vitello è (better).
c Fa (more) caldo qui (than) a casa.
d Però non fa (as hot as) l'anno scorso.
e Io mangio (less than) mio marito.

▼ Possessives ('my' and 'mine', 'your' and 'yours', etc.)

When the possessive word stands alongside the noun, it acts as an adjective, since it describes the noun by saying to whom it belongs: '**my** house', '**your** umbrella', '**her** gloves', etc.

When, however, it is separated from the noun, or when the noun does not appear at all, then it acts as a pronoun, since it takes the place of the noun: 'The house is **mine**'; 'Is this umbrella **yours**?'; 'Whose gloves are these? **Hers**'. In Italian, the same form is used for both purposes:

Questa non è **la mia** borsa – **la mia** è nera.	*This is not my handbag – mine is black.*

In Italian, the possessive always agrees with the gender and number of the noun to which it refers, not with the identity of the owner (unlike English, which distinguishes between 'his', 'her' and 'its').

La m<u>a</u>cchina viene con **la sua** garanzia.	*The car comes with its warranty.*
Lei ha **il suo** gelato e lui ha **la sua** sigaretta.	*She has her ice-cream and he has his cigarette.*

These are the different forms of the possessive in Italian:

Masc. sing.	Masc. pl.	Fem. sing.	Fem. pl.	
il mio	i miei	la mia	le mie	*my, mine*
il tuo	i tuoi	la tua	le tue	*your, yours*
il suo	i suoi	la sua	le sue	*his* *her, hers* *its* *your, yours*
il nostro	i nostri	la nostra	le nostre	*our, ours*
il vostro	i vostri	la vostra	le vostre	*your, yours*
il loro	i loro	la loro	le loro	*their, theirs*

Note: **loro** never changes.

▼ *Use of the article with possessives*
The article (**il**, **la**, etc.) is always used:

la mia borsa = *my handbag*
il suo amico = *his (or her, or your) friend*
la loro casa = *their house*

Questo è **il tuo** passaporto . . . dov'è il mio?	*This is your passport . . . where is mine?*
Andiamo **nella nostra** m<u>a</u>cchina o prendiamo la vostra?	*Shall we go in our car or shall we take yours?*

Common exception
The article is not used when referring to a member of your family, but only in the singular:

mia sorella = *my sister*	le mie sorelle = *my sisters*
suo zio = *his (or her, or your) uncle*	i suoi zii = *his (or her, or your) uncles*

The article is always used with **loro**:

il loro fratello = *their brother*

But:
The article may be left out when the sense of belonging is being stressed:

È **mio** questo bicchiere? No, è **mio** . . . ecco **il suo**.	*Is this my glass? No, it's mine . . . here's yours.*
Mi dispiace, signora, ma questo posto è **mio**.	*I'm sorry, madam, but this seat is mine.*

The indefinite article (**un**, **una**) is used with the possessive to give the meaning 'of mine', 'of his', etc.:

un mio amico = *a friend of mine* (one of my friends)
una sua cugina = *a cousin of his/hers/yours*

■ **'Suo'**

As we have seen, **suo** can refer to 'his', 'her', 'its' and also 'your'. It means 'your' when it is related to the 'you' meaning of **Lei** (the form that is used when you are not on first-name terms with a person). Sometimes the 'you' form of **suo** is written with a capital, i.e. **Suo**. Although this seems confusing, the meaning is usually clear from the context of the conversation or the text. However, in conversation, it is quite easy to confirm what is meant if need be by using the question '**di chi?**', to which the answer is '**di lui**' or **di lei**', or **di** + name.

– Ho trovato **il suo** biglietto.	– *I found his/her/your ticket.*
– Il biglietto **di chi?**	– *Whose ticket?*
– **Di Lei**, signore.	– *Yours, sir.*

▼ *Position*

The possessive almost always comes before the noun, but in idiomatic Italian it can be used after the noun for emphasis:

Faccia come in **casa sua**.	*Make yourself at home.*
Questi sono **affari miei**.	*That is my business.*
Mamma mia! = *Oh, mother!*	Dio mio! = *My God!*
(exclamation of surprise)	

▼ Activity 4   *Possessives*

Translate into Italian the words in brackets.

a Le presento (my) moglie, (my) figlio e (his) amico Mario.
b Dove sono (our) passaporti?
c Buona sera, signori. (Your) tavola è pronta.
d (Their) casa è molto bella.
e Ecco (your) valigia, signore.

▼ Demonstratives (or indicators): 'this' and 'that', 'these' and 'those'

The words for 'this' and 'that' (and their plural forms) act in the same way as any adjectives, in that they agree with the noun they accompany:

	Masc. sing.	Masc. pl.	Fem. sing.	Fem. pl.
this	questo	questi	questa quest'	queste
that	quel quell' quello	quei quegli	quella quell'	quelle

Note: the masculine singular and plural forms of **quel** behave in the same way as the definite article.

questo gelato = *this ice cream*
questa torta = *this tart*
quest'aranciata = *this orangeade*
quel melone = *that melon*
quell'arrosto = *that roast*
quella pizza = *that pizza*
quell'insalata = *that salad*

questi biscotti = *these biscuits*
queste patate = *these potatoes*

quei fichi = *those figs*
quegli spinaci = *that spinach*
(spinach is plural in Italian)
quelle cotolette = *those cutlets*

When 'that' or 'those' is a pronoun standing in for a masculine noun, the forms **quello** and **quelli** are used:

Che vino è **quello**?
Quelli sono migliori

What wine is that?
Those are better.

Note: when you want to say 'the (adjective) one' you use **quello**, and it agrees with the noun you are referring to:

Quale macchina – **quella rossa**?
L'albergo Belvedere, **quello** in via Cavour.
I vini francesi sono buoni, ma preferisco **quelli italiani**.

Which car – the red one?
The hotel Belvedere, the one in via Cavour.
French wines are good, but I prefer Italian ones.

■ **Indefinite 'that'**

In Italian, **questo** is used on its own to denote an idea or something which is not definite, where English tends to use the word 'that':

questo è vero = *that's true*
questo è ridicolo = *that's ridiculous*
ha detto questo? = *did he say that?*

You can also use **quello**:

quello è vero

▼ 'The same'

- The most common way to say 'the same' is **lo stesso** (**la stessa**, **gli stessi**, **le stesse**), using the masculine articles **lo** and **gli** because of the 'st' beginning.

lo stesso albergo = *the same hotel*
la stessa camera = *the same room*

- **Lo stesso** is also used in the indefinite sense:

è lo stesso/fà lo stesso = *it's all the same/it doesn't matter*

- **Stesso** placed after the noun is used for emphasis:

Ho parlato con il proprietario stesso. *I spoke with the owner himself.*
Abbiamo la ricevuta stessa. *We have the actual receipt (the receipt itself).*

but

Abbiamo la stessa ricevuta. *We have the same receipt.*

- **Medesimo** also means 'same', but is slightly less common than **stesso** and is used in a more deliberate sense.

Questa è **la medesima** firma. *This is the same signature.*

▼ 'The same . . . as'

This follows the same pattern as 'more than' and 'less than':

Andiamo allo stesso ristorante di ieri? *Shall we go to the same restaurant as yesterday?*

Il sistema è lo stesso in Italia che in Inghilterra.

The system is the same in Italy as in England.

but it is quite common to hear **come** instead of **di** or **che**:

lo stesso come ieri
lo stesso come in Inghilterra

▼ Quantity: 'much', 'many', 'all'

- The usual word for 'much'/'many' is **molto**.

molto, -a = *much, a lot of*
molti, -e = *many, a lot of*

moltissimo, -a = *very much*
moltissimi, -e = *very many*

But:
tanto (-a)/**tanti** (-e), (= 'so much'/'so many') is often used instead of **molto** (-a)/**molto** (-e) to mean simply 'much'/'many'.

- 'Too much'/'too many' in Italian is **troppo**(-a)/**troppi** (-e):

C'era **molta** gente alla partita?

Were there a lot of people at the match?

Sì, **tanta** . . . **moltissima**. Infatti, c'era **troppa** gente.
C'è **troppo** zucchero in questo caffè.

Yes, a lot . . . very many. In fact there were too many people.
There is too much sugar in this coffee.

- To say 'little' or 'few', use **poco**, (**poca, pochi, poche** – note 'ch' before 'i' or 'e' to keep the 'k' sound).

pochissimo, -a = *very little*
Ho mandato **pochissime** cartoline questa volta.

pochissimi, -e = *very few*
I have sent very few postcards this time.

Note: **un po' di** (or **un pochino di**) = 'a little':

Abbiamo poco tempo.
Abbiamo un po' di tempo.
Vuole **un po'** di formaggio?
Sì, ma **poco**.
Il vino è buono . . . vuole **un pochino**?

We have little (not much) time.
We have a little time.
Would you like a little cheese?
Yes, but not much.
The wine is good . . . do you want a little?

- **Tutto** (-a)/**tutti** (-e) = 'all', 'every'. These are always used with the definite article before the noun:

Ho speso **tutti i** soldi.	*I have spent all the money.*
Hai bevuto **tutta la** bottiglia?	*Have you drunk the whole bottle?*
Veniamo qui **tutte le** sere (ogni sera).	*We come here every evening.*

■ 'Ogni'

ogni (= 'each', 'every') is used only in the singular and never changes its form:

ogni giorno = *every day*
ogni sera = *every evening*
ogni volta = *every time*

▼ *Tutti: 'Everyone'*

Tutti on its own means 'everyone' and, unlike English, is plural:

tutti sono qui = *everyone is here (all are here)*

but the alternative, **ognuno** (= 'everyone'), is in the singular:

ognuno è qui = *everyone is here*

The opposite is **nessuno** (= 'no-one'), which is singular:

nessuno è qui = *no-one (nobody) is here*

All of the above adjectives of quantity, when used in the masculine singular, take on an indefinite meaning:

molto = 'a lot'
C'è molto da vedere?	*Is there a lot to see?*

Tanto = 'a lot', 'so much'
È tanto!	*It's a lot!*
No, non tanto!	*No, not so much!*

troppo = 'too much'
Non posso più . . . è troppo!	*I can't stand any more . . . it's too much.*

➤

> **poco = 'not much', 'little'**
> Ho mangiato poco oggi.   *I have not eaten much today.*
>
> **tutto = 'everything', 'all'**
> Però abbiamo visto tutto.   *But we have seen everything.*

▼ Activity 5   *Comparison and quantity*

Translate into Italian:

a Those tomatoes (*pomodori*) are too small. These are better.
b Are they not the same? No, they are much bigger.
c Is everything ready (*pronto*)? Let's all go.

▼ Interrogative adjectives

The common interrogative (or question) adjectives are:

- **che** = 'what?' (which does not change its form to agree with the noun):

che tempo fà? = *what is the weather like?*
che via è questa? = *what street is this?*
che sigarette sono quelle? = *what cigarettes are those?*

- **quale** (plural **quali**) = 'which?':

Quale numero di scarpe porta, signora?   *Which size of shoes do you take, madam?*
Quali sono le sue bambine   *Which are your little girls?*
Qual'è la prima?   *Which is the first?*

- **quanto** (-a, -i, -e) = 'how much?', 'how many?':

Quanto tempo restate?   *How long (how much time) are you staying?*

Quanti amici vengono stasera?   *How many friends are coming tonight?*

Quante volte venite in Italia?   *How often (how many times) do you come to Italy?*

Note: **quant'è?** = 'how much is it?' (It is also quite usual to say **quanto è?**)

▼ Activity 6   *Using adjectives*

Translate the words in brackets in the conversation:

– Avete una camera (big), per caso?
– Certo, signorina, (all our) camere sono (big).
– È per (my) genitori.
– Per (how much) tempo? (More than) una settimana?
– No, (less). Tre giorni, se (all) va bene.

▼ Activity 7   *Using adjectives*

Fill in the blanks with a suitable word from the box below. Each word in the box is used only once.

Al ristorante

– . . . . sembra un . . . . ristorante. C'è . . . . gente, la carta è . . . . con piatti . . . . .
– Sì, e costa . . . . .
– Io prendo le lasagne . . . . . E tu?
– Io prendo . . . . . Vuoi . . . . vino?
– Sì, ... vino è . . . .?
– È . . . . vino locale.
– È . . . .?
– È . . . . . I . . . . vini sono . . . . buoni . . . . i vini . . . ., spesso anche . . . . .
– Allora, salute! E . . . . appetito!

buon<u>i</u>ssima	un po' di	verdi	quello	questo
un nostro	che	nostri	diversi	buono
bel	buon	lo stesso	<u>o</u>ttimo	molta
tanto . . . quanto	poco	francesi	migliori	

■ **Describing quantities**

This explanation is included here as most descriptions of quantities, though not all, involve adjectives.

▼ 'Some', 'any'

There are different ways of saying 'some' or 'any' in Italian:

▼ *Using 'Del', 'della', 'dei', etc.*

This is used when the 'some' is an indefinite quantity, not something that can be counted, and when it can be easily left out in English:

Voglio comprare **del pane**.	*I want to buy (some) bread.*
Ci sono **delle belle scarpe** nella vetrina.	*There are (some) beautiful shoes in the window.*
Avete **dei guanti** in cuoio per favore?	*Have you (any) leather gloves, please?*
Abbiamo **della fortuna**.	*We are in luck.*
Ha **del coraggio**.	*He has courage.*

You can also leave it out in Italian when you mean something quite definite:

Vado a comprarmi scarpe e guanti.	*I'm going to buy myself shoes and gloves.*

▼ *Qualche*

This word means 'some' or 'any' in the sense of 'a few' or 'several'. It can also have the sense of 'some . . . or other'. It is never used with 'uncountable' nouns. It does not change its form and can be used only with a **singular** noun, even if the meaning in English is in the plural.

La vedo **qualche volta** a **qualche ricevimento**.	*I see her sometimes at some reception or other.*
C'è **qualche posto** libero?	*Are there any seats free?*

➤

▼ *Alcuni/alcune*

This is the most definite of the words used for the English 'some' or 'any'. It is used in the plural with nouns in the plural, and agrees in number and gender (it is in fact an adjective):

Abbiamo mandato **alcune cartoline** stamattina.	*We sent a number of postcards this morning.*

It cannot be used in the negative, when you must use the forms shown below.

Other plural adjectives than can translate the English 'some' are:

- **diversi**, **diverse** – which carries the sense of 'various'
- **parecchi**, **parecchie** – which carries the sense of 'many'.

▼ *Un po' di* = 'a little (of)', 'a bit of'

It is often more suitable to use **un po' di** with 'uncountable nouns' (such as 'sugar', 'milk', 'bread', 'wool', etc.) rather than **del** etc. It is more natural to say '**un po' di zucchero**' rather than '**dello zucchero**'. You can also say **un pochino di** (see suffixes on page 21) or **un poco di** (the full form of **po'**, not much used now).

Mi dia **un po' d'acqua** per cortesia.	*Give me some (a little) water, please.*

▼ *Negatives:* 'none', 'any'

When you are saying something in the negative, you cannot use **del** etc. or **alcuni**, **alcune**. You have to use either nothing at all:

Non ci sono biglietti.	*There are no tickets (there aren't any tickets).*

or **nessun** (**nessuno**, **nessuna**), but only with a **singular** noun:

Non c'è **nessun** biglietto.	*There are no tickets.*

(You may also see **alcuno**, but this is not used much now.)

➤

But: you cannot use **nessuno** with a noun which has no plural form (i.e. so-called 'uncountable' nouns):

Mi dispiace, ma **non c'è burro**.	*I'm sorry, but there isn't any butter.*
Non c'è latte per il bambino.	*There's no milk for the child.*

Remember the pronoun **ne** (see page 68):

C'è del latte per il bambino?	*Is there any milk for the child?*
No, **non ce n'è**.	*No there isn't (any).*

▼ Activity 8 *Quantities*

Try putting the following into Italian. You have already come across most of the words, but some have been put in to help you.

a There are some mistakes (*errori*) on the bill. We had (*abbiamo avuto*) some red wine but (*ma*) we did not order (*non abbiamo ordinato*) any mineral water.

b There are some lovely things (*cose*) in the cathedral (*la cattedrale*). A number of pictures (*quadri*) are by Giotto.

c I want (*voglio*) some bread and a few rolls.

d I've seen ridiculous (*esagerato*) prices in some shops.

e We don't have any intention of coming.

▼▼▼

ADVERBS
describing where, when and how something is done

Adverbs tell us how or when or where something is done. In other words, they add to the meaning of a verb. They come in various forms.

In English, the easiest adverbs to recognise are words ending in '-ly' (e.g. 'cheerfully'). Sometimes we use a whole phrase to do the same job (e.g. 'in a cheerful manner'). Often, adverbs add meaning not to a verb but to an adjective (e.g. 'very cheerful'), or to another adverb (e.g. 'too cheerfully'). However, you do not really need to know that words like 'very' and 'too' are adverbs: they are just simple words to be learned and used. It's exactly the same in Italian.

▼ Telling 'how': adverbs of manner

▼ *The ending '-mente'*
The equivalent to '-ly' in Italian is the ending '-**mente**'. To form an adverb, you simply add '-**mente**' to the **feminine singular** form of an adjective:

Adjective (fem. sing.)	Adverb	Meaning
allegra	allegramente	*cheerfully*
triste	tristemente	*sadly*

Common exception

leggera	leggermente	*lightly, slightly*

But:
When an adjective ends in a vowel + '-**le**' or '-**re**', you drop the final '-**e**' before adding '-**mente**':

formale	formalmente	*formally*
regolare	regolarmente	*regularly*

▼ *Irregular forms*

Note that

- **buono** (= 'good') becomes **bene** (= 'well')
- **cattivo** (= 'bad') becomes **male** (= 'badly').

▼ Activity 1 *Forming adverbs from adjectives*

Make adverbs ending in '-mente' from the following adjectives:

a libero (= *free, at liberty*)
b franco (= *frank*)
c onesto (= *honest*)
d facile (= *easy*)
e semplice (= *easy, simple*)
f gratuito (= *free of charge*)
g dolce (= *sweet*)
h probabile (= *probable*)
i difficile (= *difficult*)
j tenero (= *tender*)

▼ *Using adverbial phrases*

Not every adjective can have '-**mente**' added to it to make an adverb. You cannot add it to **vecchio** (= 'old'), **giovane** (= 'young'), **caro** (= 'dear') or **fresco** (= 'fresh', 'cool'), among others. This is true in English as well: for example, we cannot add '-ly' to 'difficult'. So, just as in English we use phrases such as 'with difficulty', or 'in a difficult way', in Italian too, adverbs can come in the form of phrases. The three most common are:

in (un) modo + adjective (masculine) = 'in a ... way'
in (un) modo sincero = *in a sincere way*

in (una) maniera + adjective (feminine) = 'in a ... manner'
in (una) maniera sincera = *in a sincere manner*

con + noun = 'with' + noun
con sincerità = *with sincerity*

You can also say **sinceramente**. Often, however, a phrase is used instead of the adverb ending in '-**mente**' to avoid any clumsiness, especially with longer words:

in modo intelligente = *in an intelligent way*

or when two or more adverbs come together:

Parlava **lentamente** e **con chiarezza**.   *He spoke slowly and clearly.*

▼ Activity 2   *Adverbial phrases*

Use phrases instead of the adverbs ending in '-mente' in the following:

a Lei cucina squisitamente.
b Ci accoglie amichevolmente.
c Parla francamente.
d Dice la verità apertamente.
e Annuncia autorevolmente le ultime pettegolezze (= 'gossip').

▼ *Using adjectives as adverbs*

Often, instead of adding the ending '-**mente**' or using a phrase, you can simply use the appropriate adjective (remembering to make it agree with the subject):

cantavano allegri = *they sang cheerfully*

Some adjectives are used in the masculine singular as adverbs (see also page 39):

cantavano piano = *they sang softly*
ridevano forte = *they laughed loudly*
mangiavano molto = *they ate a lot*
bevevano troppo = *they drank too much*

Remember that **molto** can mean 'very' and **troppo** can mean 'too':

molto forte = *very loudly*
troppo forte = *too loudly*

▼ Telling 'how' or 'how much': adverbs of quantity

Most common adverbs of quantity are not based on adjectives.

abbastanza = enough

| Ho mangiato abbastanza. | *I've eaten enough.* |

appena = just

| È appena arrivato | *He's just arrived* |

appena = scarcely, hardly

| È appena abbastanza. | *It's scarcely enough.* |

meno = less

| Costa meno. | *It costs less.* |

parecchio = a lot

| Costa parecchio. | *It costs a lot.* |

non ... più = not any more, no longer

| Non lo fanno più. | *They don't make it any more.* |

piuttosto = rather

| È piuttosto caro. | *It's rather/somewhat expensive.* |

poco = not very, little

| È poco conosciuto. | *It's not very well known.* |

quasi = almost, nearly

| È quasi finito. | *It's almost finished.* |

▼ Telling 'when': adverbs of time

A few adverbs of time can be made up from adjectives, e.g. **immediatamente** (= 'immediately'), **finalmente** (= 'finally'), **raramente** (= 'rarely'), but most are words which just have to be learned. Here are some of the most common in everyday use:

| oggi = *today* | spesso = *often* |
| ieri = *yesterday* | subito = *at once* |

domani = *tomorrow*
ora = *now*
allora = *then*
finora = *until now*
adesso = *now*
prima = *before, previously*
dopo = *after, afterwards*
poi = *next, then*
sempre = *always*
mai = *never*

fra/tra poco = *soon*
talvolta (qualche volta) = *sometimes*
adagio = *slowly*
presto = *quickly, early*
già = *already*
tardi = *late (in the day)*
in ritardo = *late (behind time)*
prima o poi = *sooner or later*
più che mai = *more than ever*

▼ Telling 'where': adverbs of place

Many adverbs of place are simply prepositions without a following noun, such as:

dentro = *inside*
fuori = *outside*
davanti = *in front*
dietro = *behind*
su = *up*

sopra = *above*
sotto = *below*
vicino = *near*
lontano = *far*

Guarda fuori.

Guarda fuori **della finestra**.

Look outside (adverb).

Look out of the window (preposition).

Other common ones are:

dovunque/ovunque = *everywhere, anywhere*
altrove = *elsewhere*
dappertutto = *everywhere*

Note: there is no single word for 'nowhere' – you have to say **da nessuna parte**.

■ Here and there

'Here' is either **qui** or **qua**.
'There' is either **lì** or **là**.

Nowadays, there is no real difference in meaning between the two forms and you can use either:

vieni qui/vieni qua = *come here*
sono lì/sono là = *they are there*

➤

Qua and **là** join up with **su** and **giù** to make:

quassù = *up here*   lassù = *up there*
quaggiù = *down here*   laggiù = *down there*

Note the stress mark over the 'u', and the doubling of the 's' of **su** and the 'g' of **giù**.

You can use **qui** or **qua** and **lì** or **là** before other adverbs of place:

qui/qua vicino = *near here*   là/lì dentro = *in there*

▼ Position of adverbs

Adverbs are usually placed directly after the verb in everyday Italian, although you may see them in other positions for reasons of style or emphasis.

Cominciamo **bene**, siamo **già in ritardo!**	*We're starting well, we're already late!*

They never come between the subject and the verb, unlike in English:

Io vado **sempre** allo stesso ristorante.	*I always go to the same restaurant.*

In compound tenses (see Verbs, page 97), the adverb usually comes after the whole tense:

Ho mangiato **bene** in questo ristorante.	*I've eaten well in this restaurant.*

but a few (such as **sempre, mai, quasi, ancora, appena, già**) can come either between or after the two parts of the verb:

Ho sempre mangiato bene in questo ristorante.	*I've always eaten well in this restaurant.*

or

Ho mangiato sempre bene in questo ristorante.

▼ More or less: comparison of adverbs

This is done in exactly the same way as with adjectives (see pages 29–32), using **più**, **il più**, and **meno**, **il meno**:

Può parlare più lentamente, per cortesia?	*Can you speak more slowly, please?*
Capisco l'accento napoletano meno facilmente che quello milanese.	*I understand the Neapolitan accent less easily than the Milanese one.*
Per favore, parlate il più piano possibile – il bambino dorme.	*Please speak as quietly as possible – the baby is sleeping.*

▼ *The absolute superlative: '-issimamente'*

You can add the adverb ending '**-mente**' to adjectives ending in '**-issima**' (remembering to use the feminine form of the adjective):

Parlava **rapidissimamente**.	*He spoke very quickly.*

But, as you can see, this is often quite clumsy, so the usual thing to do is to use **molto + adverb/adjective/noun**:

Parlava **molto rapidamente**.

or

Parlava **in modo molto rapido**.	Parlava **con molta rapidità**.

However, it is very common to use the '**-issimo**' ending on **molto** (**moltissimo**) and **poco** (**pochissimo**) when they are used alone as adverbs, and with **bene** (**benissimo**), and **male** (**malissimo**):

Questo vestito mi piace **moltissimo**.	*I like this dress very much.*
Ti va **benissimo**.	*It suits you very well. (It goes very well on you.)*

Note: **troppo** never changes. If you want to say more than 'too much', you have to add something like **veramente** (= 'really'):

È veramente troppo. = *It's really too much.*

▼ *As . . . as possible – il più (meno) . . . possibile*

This is a way of expressing the relative superlative with an adverb.

Verrò il più presto possibile.	*I'll come as quickly (as soon) as possible.*

(Another common way to say this is 'al più presto' – 'verrò al più presto'.)

L'ho spiegato il più chiaramente possibile.	*I explained it as clearly as possible.*
L'ho spiegato nel modo più chiaro.	
La vedo il meno possibile.	*I see her as little as possible.*

■ **'Bene' and 'male'**

Adjective	Adverb	Comparative adverb	Superlative adverb
buono/a *good*	bene *well*	meglio *better*	il meglio *(the) best*
cattivo/a *bad*	male *badly*	peggio *worse*	il peggio *(the) worst*

• **Bene** and **male** are used when talking about one's health:

sto bene = *I am well*	mi sento male = *I feel ill*
Stai meglio adesso?	*Are you better now?*
Dice che sua mamma sta peggio.	*He says his mother is worse.*

Note that the verb used for health is always **stare** and never **essere** (see Verbs, page 95).

• They are also used in some common impersonal expressions:

– **Sarebbe bene** scendere qui?	– *Would it be as well to get off here?*
– No, **è meglio** scendere alla prossima fermata.	– *No, it's better to get off at the next stop.*
– **Va bene**, ma **il peggio** è che piove fortissimo.	– *OK, but the worst of it is that it's raining very heavily.*
– **Peggio per noi!**	– *So much the worse for us!*
– No, **peggio per te** . . . io ho l'impermeabile, e tu no!	– *No, hard luck on you . . . I've got my raincoat and you haven't!*

▼ Activity 3 *Using adverbs*

Translate the adverbs in brackets into Italian:

a Andiamo (inside) perchè è (already late).
b Andate (directly) alla stazione. Vi raggiungeremo (as soon as) possibile.
c Mi va (well) la minigonna? Dimmi (honestly).
d Non sò (exactly). Forse sarebbe (better) prenderla (slightly) più lunga.
e Detto (very delicately) e (diplomatically)! Ma parla (more quietly)!

▼▼▼

PRONOUNS
replacements for nouns

▼ Personal pronouns

In the films, Tarzan speaks only primitive English, so he says things like 'Tarzan love Jane'. If he were not so primitive, he might replace the noun 'Tarzan' with the pronoun 'I' and the noun 'Jane' with the pronoun 'you', finishing up with 'I love you'. And when he says 'Jane love Tarzan', he might replace 'Jane' with the pronoun 'you' and 'Tarzan' with the pronoun 'me'. So his line would be, 'I love you – you love me.'

'I' and 'you' (along with 'he', 'she', 'it', 'we', 'you' (plural) and 'they') are known as **personal pronouns**, since they stand for individuals (whether named or not and whether human or not).

'Me' is also a personal pronoun (together with 'him', 'her', 'it', 'us', 'you' and 'them').

The two groups consist of different words (except for 'it' and 'you', which stay the same) because they have different roles in the sentence.

In 'I love you', 'I' (in this case Tarzan) is the one doing the loving, and 'you' (Jane) is being loved (the object of love). So:

- 'I' is the **subject pronoun** (in charge of the verb 'love')
- 'you' is the **object pronoun** (the object of the verb 'love').

In 'you love me':

- 'you' becomes the subject of the verb – the **subject pronoun**
- 'me' is the object of the verb – the **object pronoun**.

▼ *Subject pronouns: 'I', 'you', 'he', etc.*
Here are the subject personal pronouns in Italian. Note that first person refers to the person(s) speaking, second person refers to the person(s) being spoken to, and third person refers to the person(s) or thing(s) being spoken about.

io	*I*
tu	*you*
lui	*he*
lei	*she*
Lei	*you* (polite form)
noi	*we*
voi	*you*
loro	*they*
Loro	*you* (plural polite form)

The following forms are rarely used in normal everyday speech and writing, but you will see them in books and in some styles of journalism and you may hear them in some more formal types of speech:

esso	*he, it*
essa	*she*
egli	*he*
ella	*she*
essi	*they*
esse	*they*

■ 'You'

- If you are on familiar or first-name terms with a person, use the **tu** form and its plural **voi**.
- If you are not on first name terms with a person, use the **Lei** form. This is in fact the third person form and takes the third person form of the verb. Several centuries ago, **eccellenza** ('excellency') came into normal use as a respectful form of address and, since the noun was feminine, the pronoun taking its place was feminine as well – formerly **ella** and now **Lei**.
- The plural of **Lei** is, strictly speaking, **Loro** (third person plural), but this is now quite formal, and the plural most used now is **Voi**.
- **Lei** is often (but not necessarily) spelled with a capital 'L'. It will be printed in this book with a capital L to avoid confusion with **lei** ('she'). **Voi** is also often spelled with a capital (especially in business correspondence). ➤

- Even though **Lei** is a feminine form of pronoun, it is treated as a masculine when you are addressing a male person. So you would say:

Lei è occupato, signore? *Are you busy, sir?*

The grammatical genders here have nothing to do with sex – or political correctness!

Subject pronouns in Italian are normally used only when you want to emphasise or make clear who the subject is. Otherwise, the form of the verb is enough to tell you. For example, **noi andiamo** means 'we are going', but unless you want to emphasise 'we' it is enough just to say **andiamo**.

Andiamo al cinema. *We're going to the cinema.*
Noi andiamo al cinema ma **loro** no. *We're going to the cinema, but they're not.*

A very common way of emphasising is to put the subject pronoun after the verb:

Aspetta un momento – lo faccio **io**. *Wait a minute – I'll do it.*
Paga **lui**! *He's paying!*

▼ *Object pronouns: 'me', 'you', 'him', etc.*
There are two kinds of object – the direct and the indirect:

- In 'he marries her', the pronoun 'her' is the direct object of the verb 'marries' (the one being married).

- In 'he gives her a wedding ring', the pronoun 'her' is an indirect object; it is a shortened form of 'to/for her'.

In English, the subject pronoun comes in front of the verb and the object pronoun(s) come after the verb.

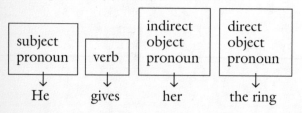

In Italian, both the subject and the object pronoun(s) come in front of the verb (with the exception of the form **loro** which comes after the verb).

Here are the object pronouns in Italian:

	Singular		**Plural**	
	Direct	**Indirect**	**Direct**	**Indirect**
1st Pers.	mi – *me*	mi – *(to) me*	ci – *us*	ci – *(to) us*
2nd Pers.	ti – *you*	ti – *(to) you*	vi – *you*	vi – *(to) you*
3rd Pers.	lo – *him (it)*	gli – *(to) him (it)*	li – *them*	[2]gli – *(to) them*
				[3]loro – *(to) them*
	la – *her (it)*	le – *(to) her (it)*	le – *them (f)*	[3]loro – *(to) them (f)*
	La – *you*	Le – *(to) you*	[1]Vi – *you*	Vi – *(to) you*
				Loro – *(to) you*

Examples:

Ti compro un gelato.	*I'll buy you an ice-cream. (i.e. for you)*
Quella giacca **le** sta bene.	*That jacket suits her.*
Le posso offrire da bere?	*Can I offer you a drink?*
Loro **ci** hanno mandato i biglietti.	*They sent us the tickets.*
Vi ringrazio molto.	*Thank you very much.*
Non **li** vedo molto bene in questa luce.	*I can't see them very well in this light.*
Vi auguro un Buon Natale a tutti.	*I wish you all a happy Christmas.*

Note the following points:

- **La** and **lo** change to **l'** before a vowel, and before the initial 'h' in parts of the verb **avere** (= 'to have'). However, they often keep the full form before an 'i':

lo imparo/l'imparo = *I am learning it*

- **Mi**, **ti**, **ci** and **vi** may drop the 'i' to become **m'**, **t'**, **c'** and **v'** before 'a', 'e', 'o', 'u' or initial 'h', but this is optional:

M'aiuta/Mi aiuta.	*Help me.*
Lui **mi** ama, ma io l'odio.	*He loves me, but I hate him.*
L'ho visto ieri.	*I saw him yesterday.*

but they always drop the 'i' before another 'i':

m'ingrasso = *I'm putting on weight* c'informa = *he informs us*

- **Gli** is now the most usual indirect object pronoun in the masculine plural, but for the feminine plural **loro** is normally used. **Loro** always comes after the verb:

Mando **loro** una cartolina.	*I'm sending them a postcard.*
Ho regalato **loro** una bella bambola.	*I gave them a lovely doll.*
Gli scrivo una lettera.	*I'm writing them (or him) a letter.*

- Just as the usual plural of **Lei** (= 'you') is **Voi**, so the common direct and indirect object forms are **Vi**. You may still come across the polite form **Loro**, but nowadays usually only in the indirect form.

▼ Activity 1   *Direct and indirect object pronouns*

Translate the words in brackets into Italian and use them to fill in the gaps.

a '. . . . chiamano Mimi' è un'aria bellissima, e . . . . canta bene. (me, she, it)

b Ciao, Franco, ... telefono domani. (you)

c . . . . abbiamo già dato i soldi. (to him)

d Ma non . . . . ha dato una ricevuta. (to us)

e Non . . . . importa – . . . . riceveremo domani. (to me, it)

▼ *More than one pronoun*

When two direct object pronouns come together:

- The indirect object comes first.

- **mi**, **ti**, **ci** and **vi** change to **me**, **te**, **ce** and **ve** when they come before the direct object pronouns **lo**, **la**, **li** and **le**:

Mi fa vedere?	*Will you let me see?*
Me lo fa vedere?	*Will you let me see it?*
T'insegno l'italiano.	*I'll teach you Italian.*
Te lo insegno.	*I'll teach it to you.*

Ci può cambiare questo assegno?	*Can you cash this cheque for us?*
Ce lo può cambiare?	*Can you cash it for us?*
Vi presentiamo l'<u>u</u>ltimo modello,	*We present to you the latest*
e **ve lo** offriamo ad un prezzo	*model, and we are offering it to*
speciale.	*you at a special price.*

• **Loro** (indirect object pronoun) always follows the verb, even when there are two pronouns involved:

Insegno **loro** l'italiano.	*I teach them Italian.*
Lo insegno **loro**.	*I teach it to them.*

Very often, the word **a**, meaning 'to', is put in front of **loro**, even though it is not necessary, since **loro** itself means 'to them':

Lo mando a loro.	*I send it to them.*

• When **gli** and **le** come first in a sequence of two object pronouns, they change to '**glie-**' and join up with the following pronoun to form one word. (The stress falls on the 'e' of ' **glie-**' and the sound is usually more like the 'y' in 'yes' than the 'lli' in 'million'.)

Gli faccio vedere la strada migliore.	*I'll show him the best road.*
Gliela faccio vedere	*I'll show it to him.*
Le incarto separati i collant e il	*Shall I wrap the tights and scarf*
foulard, signora?	*separately for you, madam?*
Glieli incarto separati, signora?	*Shall I wrap them separately for*
	you, madam?

▼ Activity 2   *Combining direct and indirect object pronouns*

Translate the words in brackets into Italian and use them to fill in the gaps in the following sentences.

a Il conto? .... pago domani. (it to him)
b Prendo queste scarpe. .... può tenere fino a stasera? (them for me)
c L'Albergo Belvedere – .... può raccomandare? (it to us)
d Cerco la via Cavour. .... può indicare, per cortesia? (it to me)
e Deve <u>e</u>ssere vero, se .... dici tu. (it to me)

▼ *Position of object pronouns*

As we have seen, object pronouns (with the exception of **loro**) come before the verb. However, when the verb is in the infinitive form (see page 82) the pronouns are tacked on to the end of the verb to form one word. The final 'e' of the infinitive is dropped to make way for the pronouns. The stress remains where it was before the addition:

Voglio imparare l'italiano.	*I want to learn Italian.*
Voglio **impararlo**.	*I want to learn it.*
Voglio **insegnarti** l'italiano.	*I want to teach you Italian.*
Voglio **insegnartelo***.	*I want to teach it to you.*

*Note the change of **ti** to **te** as explained above, and the running together of '**-telo**'.

▼ **Activity 3**   *Infinitive + direct/indirect object pronoun*

Now try putting the following into Italian. You have already seen these sentences in the previous exercise, but this time add the pronouns to the infinitive of the verb instead of putting them in front of it.

a I'll take these shoes. Can you keep them for me until this evening?
b The Hotel Belvedere – can you recommend it to us?
c I am looking for via Cavour. Can you point it out to me, please?

The same thing happens when the verb is in the present participle form (see page 96):

mangiandolo = *eating it*
comprandomeli = *buying me them, buying them for myself*
indicandogliela = *pointing it out to him*

It also occurs when the verb is in the command (imperative) form, but only in the second person (**tu** and **voi** forms):

Dammi la mano.	*Give me your hand.* (second person singular)
Fategli lo sconto . . . si, **fateglielo**.	*Give him the discount . . . yes, give him it.* (second person plural)

Ci faccia il conto ... per cortesia **ce lo faccia**.	*Bring us the bill ... please, bring us it.* (polite third person singular)

Note: Although the verb **fare** means 'to do' or 'to make', it is used in so many ways that you have to find different equivalents in English.

■ Ecco!

Ecco! means 'here is', 'here are', 'there is', 'there are' in the sense of pointing out something:

ecco il taxi! = *here's the taxi!*   ecco i ragazzi! = *there are the boys!*

The object pronoun joins on to it:

eccolo! = *here it is!*   eccoli! = *there they are!*
eccomi! = *here I am!*

▼ *Reflexive pronouns: '-self'*

There is another kind of object pronoun, which is called **reflexive** because it reflects back to the subject. In English, we recognise it by the ending '-self'.

The *first* and *second* person object pronouns listed on page 57 can all be used as reflexive pronouns:

Io **mi** alzo alle sette.	*I get up at seven* (get myself up).
Tu **ti** lavi le mani.	*You wash your hands* (the hands of yourself).
Noi **ci** svegliamo presto.	*We wake up early* (wake ourselves).
Voi **vi** sedete qui.	*You are sitting here* (you seat yourselves).

But:

The odd one out is the third person reflexive pronoun, which is **si** in both the singular and the plural (note that **sì** with an accent is 'yes', while the reflexive pronoun **si** is written without an accent):

Lui **si** alza alle nove.	*He gets up at nine.*
Lei **si** vanta di essere bella.	*She prides herself on being beautiful.*

Si acc_o_modi, signore.   *Sit here, sir.*
Loro **si** v_e_stono da sportivi.   *They dress in sports clothes.*
Dopo il lavoro **si** c_a_mbiano.   *After work they change (clothes).*

When **si** comes together with other object pronouns it changes to **se**, in the same way as **mi**, **ti**, **ci** and **vi**. It also works in the same way with regard to position:

Lei puo **accomodarsi** qui, signore.   *You may sit here, sir.*
Le scarpe? **Se le** cambia due volte al giorno.   *Shoes? She changes them twice a day.*

Notice that in Italian where the object belongs to the subject of the verb, then you use the reflexive pronoun instead of saying 'his', 'her', 'my', etc.:

Io **mi** lavo le mani.   *I wash my hands.*
Lui **si** cambia la cam_i_cia.   *He changes his shirt.*

Similarly, reflexive pronouns are used as indirect objects in order to create a kind of emphasis in situations where we would not use an extra pronoun in English:

Mi sono comprato un nuovo vestito.   *I have bought (myself) a new dress.*
Mi sono mangiato una bella pizza.   *I ate a lovely pizza. (I had myself a lovely pizza.)*

▼ *Reciprocal pronouns: 'each other'*
Reflexive pronouns are also used to mean 'each other' and 'one another':

(Noi) **ci** vedremo domani.   *We will see each other tomorrow.*
Mett_e_tevi d'accordo.   *Reach an agreement with each other (agree among yourselves).*

(Loro) **si** sp_o_sano in chiesa.   *They are getting married (marrying each other) in church.*

▼ Activity 4　　　　　　　　　*Reflexive pronouns*

Translate the following sentences into Italian. You will need to use reflexive pronouns and, in some cases, subject pronouns.

a　I'm putting on my shoes.
b　She is washing her hair.
c　They see each other every day.
d　I am going to do myself a favour.

▼ *Emphatic pronouns*

This is another form of object pronoun:

me	*me, myself*
te	*you, yourself*
lui	*him*
lei	*her*
sè	*himself*
	herself
	yourself (polite)
noi	*us*
voi	*you*
loro	*them*
sè	*themselves*

These are always used on their own, never attached to each other or to parts of a verb. You use them:

● to emphasise:

Chiama **me**?	*Are you calling **me**? (Is it me you're calling?)*
No, chiamo **lui**.	*No, I'm calling **him**.*

Often, the pronoun is repeated in both forms for emphasis, especially with the indirect object:

Glielo scrivo **a lui**.	*I'm writing it to him.*
Te lo dirò **a te**.	*I will tell you.*

● to distinguish or clarify:

Chiamo **lui**, non **te**.	*I'm calling him, not you.*
Pago **loro**, non **voi**.	*I'll pay them, not you.*

• after prepositions (see pages 72–80 and box):

Mi porti **con te**?	*Will you take me with you?*
Venite **con noi**.	*Come with us.*
Prega **per me**.	*Pray for me.*
Lo fa **da sè**.	*He does it by himself.*
'Fare **Da Sè**'	*'Do It Yourself' (DIY)*
Parlo **di loro**.	*I'm speaking about them.*

Note that **sè** is always reflexive, so there is a difference between:

Lo scrive per **lui**.   *He's writing it for him.*

and

Lo scrive per **sè**.   *He's writing it for himself.*

■ Preposition + emphatic pronoun

There are some prepositions which are usually followed by **di** when they come before an emphatic pronoun (but not when they come before a noun). Some of the most common are **contro** (= 'against'), **dentro** (= 'in', 'inside'), **dietro** (= 'behind'), **sopra** (= 'on', 'over', 'above'), **sotto** (= 'underneath', 'below'):

Lui sta **contro di me**.	*He is against me.*
Lo sento **dentro di me**.	*I feel it within myself.*

Senza (= 'without'); **dopo** (= 'after'); **fra** (= 'among'); and **verso** (= 'towards') are sometimes used with the preposition **di** when followed by an emphatic pronoun:

Siamo usciti **senza (di) loro**.   *We went out without them.*

The preposition **da** followed by an emphatic pronoun can have various meanings:

• 'at' (in the sense of 'at the house of' or 'at the place of'):

Venite a mangiare da noi domani.	*Come and eat at our house tomorrow.*
Qui **da noi** c'è troppa burocrazia.	*Here in our country there is too much bureaucracy.*

➤

- 'to' (again in the sense of 'to the house of'):

Andiamo **da Carla** stasera?   *Are we going to Carla's tonight?*

- 'by oneself', 'on one's own':

L'hai fatto **da te**?   *Did you do it on your own?*
L'ho imparato **da me**.   *I learned it by myself.*

(There are other meanings and uses of **da** which are explained on page 74.)

Very often **stesso** is used alongside **sè**:

Lo scrive per **se stesso**.   *He's writing it for himself.*
Lo chiede per **se stessa**.   *She's asking for it for herself.*
I clienti lo comprano per **se stessi**.   *The customers buy it for themselves.*

Note: se is usually written without the accent when it appears alongside **stesso** – for the simple reason that in this phrase it cannot be confused with **se** meaning 'if'.

■ **'It's me', etc.**
Where in English we say, 'it's me', 'it's him', etc., Italian uses the subject pronoun, not the emphatic pronoun, with the corresponding person of the verb <u>e</u>ssere:

sono io = *it's me*   siamo noi = *it's us*
sei tu = *it's you*   siete voi = *it's you* (plural)
è lui = *it's him*   sono loro = *it's them*

▼ **Activity 5**   *Emphatic pronouns*

Translate the words in brackets into Italian.

a Amo (you) non (her). Vieni con (me).
b Giocano per (themselves), non per la squadra.
c Gli spaghetti sono per (me), le tagliatelle per (them).
d La vita è cara (in your country).
e Puoi andare (on your own, without me).

▼ Impersonal pronouns

▼ *Impersonal use of 'si'*

In English we often use 'one' or 'you' in a general or impersonal sense, as in 'one can see that he is ill' or 'you pour in a cup of milk and bring to the boil'. Other words used in this vague or general sense are 'we', 'they', 'people', etc.

The Italian equivalent is to use **si** with the third person singular of the verb:

Si vede che sta male.	*One can see that he is ill.*
Si versa una tazza di latte e si porta all'ebollizione.	*You pour in a cup of milk and bring to the boil.*

Some very common phrases are:

si dice = *they say, people say, it is said.*
si vede! = *that's obvious!*
qui si mangia bene = *you eat well here*
si sta bene così = *we're fine like this*
si va? = *shall we go?*

As you can see there are many ways of translating **si** into English ('one', 'you', 'they', 'we', 'people'). Usually it is a case of deciding what we would say naturally to give the same sense as the Italian.

The use of **si** to translate the passive is explained in the section on verbs (page 105).

▼ Activity 6   *Impersonal use of 'si'*

Translate the following into English.

a Dov'è che si paga?
b Si deve andare allo sportello.
c Grazie. Si può pagare con la carta di credito?
d Certo. Oggi si vive con le carte di credito.
e Sì – e si spende troppo!

▼ *Ci*

As well as meaning 'us', **ci** is also used to mean 'there' (or 'to it'/'to them' in the sense of 'there'). It is very common. (**Vi** is also used in the same way, but is not so common in the spoken language today.)

c'è, ci sono = *there is, there are* (general, not pointing out)

C'è molto rumore là.	*There is a lot of noise there.*
Andiamo al cinema? No, non **ci** posso andare.	*Shall we go to the cinema? No, I can't go (there).*
Dammi quel foglio, **ci** metto la mia firma.	*Give me that sheet, I'll put my signature to it.*

Ci also occurs frequently in certain idiomatic expressions:

- It is very often used with the verb **avere** (= 'to have'), not with any particular meaning but mainly for the sound. Italians will always say, for example, '**ce l'hai?**' (= 'have you got it?') rather than '**l'hai?**' and reply '**sì, ce l'ho**' rather than simply '**sì, l'ho**'.

- You will also often hear '**ci sei?**' ('are you ready?') and '**ci sono**' ('I'm ready'), and, of course, the equivalents '**ci siete?**'('are you ready?'), '**ci siamo**' ('we're ready').

- It is also used to ask if someone is there (or in):

C'è qualcuno?	*Is anyone there?*
No, non **c'è** nessuno.	*No, there's nobody here.*
C'è il dottore?	*Is the doctor in?*
No, non **c'è**.	*No, he's not in.*

Ci comes after first and second person pronouns (**mi, ti, vi**), though you will **never** find the combination '**ci ci**', which is always avoided:

Loro vanno al ristorante e **mi ci** hanno invitato.	*They are going to the restaurant and they have invited me (to it).*

but it comes in front of third person pronouns, and changes to **ce**:

È vero che non **ce** l'hanno?	*Is it true that they haven't got it?*

▼ *Ne*

Ne is a pronoun which stands for 'of him', 'of her', 'of it' or 'of the'. It takes the place of **di** + noun or personal pronoun:

Lui parla spesso di sua madre.	He often speaks of (about) his mother.
Lui **ne** parla spesso.	He speaks of (about) her often.
Quante pesche vuole?	How many peaches do you want?
Ne voglio cinque.	I want five (of them).

It also has the meaning of 'some' and 'any':

Ci sono posti?	Are there seats (places)?
Sì, ce **ne** sono.	Yes, there are some.
No, non ce **ne** sono.	No, there aren't any.

Ne always comes last in a sequence of pronouns. Before **ne**, the object pronouns **mi**, **ti**, **ci** and **vi** and impersonal **ci** change their ending to '-e'. **Ne** combines with **gli** to become **gliene**:

Gliene parla spesso.	He often speaks to him about her.
Me **ne** dia cinque, per favore?	Give me five (of them), please.

▼ Activity 7 — *The pronouns 'ci' and 'ne'*

Fill in the blanks using 'ci', 'ce', 'c'è', 'ci sono' or 'ne' as appropriate.

a Vuole giornali inglesi, ma non .... abbiamo.
b .... un posto libero? No, non ....
c Vieni alla partita? .... andiamo tutti.
d Lei conosce il dottor Loversi. .... abbiamo parlato ieri.
e .... gelati da duemila lire? Sì, quanti .... vuole?

▼ Possessives: 'mine', 'yours', etc.

In Italian, these are practically the same as possessive adjectives, 'my', 'your', etc. – **il mio, la tua**, etc. (see pages 33–35).

▼ Demonstrative pronouns: 'this', 'that', etc.

Again, these are practically the same as the demonstrative adjectives, which are dealt with on page 36.

▼ Relative pronouns: 'who', 'which', 'that', 'whose', etc.

These are words which link one part of a sentence to another by relating back to a noun already mentioned. In English, we use the words 'which', 'that', 'who', 'whom' etc., depending on the noun being referred to and its function in the sentence.

In Italian, this job is done by two simple words, which do not change to agree with the noun:

- To refer back to any subject or direct object, you use the word **che**:

la musica **che** suonava	*the music which was playing*
la casa **che** ha costruito Jack	*the house that Jack built*
la donna **che** ha aperto la porta	*the woman who opened the door*
la gente **che** abbiamo visto	*the people (whom) we saw*
l'uomo **che** amo	*the man (whom) I love*

Note: unlike some English relative pronouns, **che** is never missed out.

- After a preposition you use **cui**:

Dov'è il ristorante **di cui** parlava?	*Where is the restaurant you were speaking of?*
Questa è la persona **da cui** abbiamo comprato i biglietti.	*This is the person from whom we bought the tickets.*
Quello è il negozio **in cui** siamo entrati.	*That is the shop we went into (into which we went).*
Questa è la foto del cugino **(a) cui** mando la cartolina.*	*This is the photo of the cousin to whom I'm sending the postcard.*

*Note that **cui** also means 'to him', etc., so you do not need to put the preposition **a** in front of it.

• When you use the definite article with **cui**, it has the meaning of 'whose'. The definite article agrees with the thing that belongs, not the owner:

Questo è il bambino **il cui compleanno** festeggiamo.
This is the child whose birthday we are celebrating.

Questo è il signore **la cui figlia** conosciamo.
This is the gentleman whose daughter we know.

• An alternative to **che** and **cui** is **il quale** (**la quale**, **i quali**, **le quali**):

la donna **la quale** ha aperto la porta
the woman who opened the door

but you would only use it in everyday conversation to make absolutely clear whom you are referring to, in case of doubt:

Ho visto la sorella di Jack, **la quale** m'ha detto . . .
I saw Jack's sister, who told me . . .

There is no confusion in English, because of the position of the words, but there could be in Italian, where **che** could refer to either **la sorella** or to Jack.

Il quale is also used instead of **cui** after prepositions:

Questa è la persona **dalla quale** abbiamo comprato i biglietti.
Quello è il negozio **nel quale** siamo entrati.
Questa è la foto del cugino **al quale** mando la cartolina.

▼ *'What' ('that which')*
When we say in English, for example, 'I don't understand what he's saying', the word 'what' is a relative pronoun meaning 'that which'. In Italian, you use **quello che** or **ciò che**:

Non capisco **quello che** dice.   Non capisco **ciò che** dice.

You will also hear '**Non capisco quel che dice**.' **Quel** is an alternative to **quello**, but until you have the 'feel' of the language it is better to use **quello che**:

Quello che (**ciò che**) mi piace qui è il clima.
What I like here is the climate.

Lei può ordinare **quello che** (**ciò che**) vuole.
You can order what you want.

Note: **quello che** and **ciò che** refer to indefinite ideas or things, exactly as the word 'what' does in English. They do not refer back to a noun, and so their form does not vary.

▼ Activity 8

Translate this passage into Italian. You may need to refer to the explanation of demonstrative adjectives on page 36 as well as the notes on pronouns, above.

- Let's go to that shop in which we saw those lovely handbags yesterday. Can you buy one (of them) for me?
- Ah, here it is!
- No, it's not this shop, it's that little one. I'll go (there) by myself; you can do what you want, it doesn't matter to me.
- I would like the black handbag I saw yesterday – the large one. Mine is old, and too small. In our country there aren't any – not as nice as these. I'll take it.
- Shall I put it in gift paper (**carta da regalo**) for you?
- No – the gift is for myself . . . but he's paying!

▼▼▼
PREPOSITIONS
describing how things relate to each other

Prepositions are little words which give an indication of the position or purpose of the noun or pronoun they go with. Some of the commonest ones are **in** (= 'in'), **a** (= 'to'), **per** (= 'for'), **con** (= 'with'), **di** (= 'of') and **da** (= 'from'). Many of these join up with the definite article to form one word in the following way:

	il	lo	la	l'	i	gli	le
a (ad)	al	allo	alla	all'	ai	agli	alle
da	dal	dallo	dalla	dall'	dai	dagli	dalle
di (d')	del	dello	della	dell'	dei	degli	delle
in	nel	nello	nella	nell'	nei	negli	nelle
su	sul	sullo	sulla	sull'	sui	sugli	sulle
con	col				coi		

Note: the other forms with **con** are not normally used in everyday Italian nowadays, although you may often see them in print. The forms with **per** (**pel**, **pella**, etc.) are no longer used.

▼ Prepositions used before nouns

Although each preposition has one basic meaning, there are many idiomatic expressions in which they are used which have different equivalents in English.

▼ *a* = 'to', 'at', 'in'
A usually becomes **ad** before a vowel, although you will often hear simply **a**. Here is a list of its most common uses:

• **a** is used to mean 'to', 'at' or 'in' with names of places:

Siamo **a** Roma e andiamo **ad**
Empoli.
Non voglio stare **a casa**, voglio
andare **al** cinema.

We are in Rome and we are
going to Empoli.
I don't want to stay at home, I
want to go to the cinema.

- **a** translates 'by' in the following expressions:

fatto a mano = *made by hand, handmade*
imparato a memoria = *learned by heart*

- **a** + direction

a destra = *on the right*   a sinistra = *on the left*

- **a** + times of day

all'una = *at one o'clock*   alle (ore) sei = *at six o'clock*
alle tredici = *at 1300 hours*   a mezzanotte = *at midnight*

- **a** is used very often with a verb before the infinitive of
  another verb (see page 78):

Imparo **a** scrivere l'italiano.   *I'm learning to write Italian.*

- Some other prepositions are always used with **a** when they
  are followed by a noun:

davanti a = 'in front of'
davanti alla porta   *in front of the door*

vicino a = 'near'
vicino al mare   *near the sea*

accanto a = 'beside', 'next to'
accanto alla chiesa   *beside the church*

fino a = 'as far as', 'until'
andiamo fino alla stazione   *we're going as far as the station*
fino a mezzogiorno   *until midday*

di fronte a = 'facing', 'opposite'
di fronte alla stazione   *opposite the station*

intorno a = 'around'
intorno alla tavola   *around the table*

▼ *con* = 'with'

un'acqua minerale **con** ghiaccio	*a mineral water with ice*
Andiamo **con** la macchina?	*Shall we go by car?*

▼ *da* = 'from', 'by', 'to', 'at', 'with'

Veniamo **da** Londra.	*We come from London.*
Il conto è stato pagato **da** mio marito.	*The bill was paid by my husband.*
È andato **dal** dentista.	*He has gone to the dentist's.*
Ogni domenica mangio **da** mia mamma.	*Every Sunday I have lunch at my mother's.*
una ragazza dai capelli biondi	*a girl with fair hair*
da solo (sola, etc)	*alone, by oneself*
La ragazza è andata **da** sola.	*The girl went alone.*

Note also:

una tazza da caffè = *a coffee cup*
una camicia da notte = *a nightdress*
un biglietto da cinquemila lire = *a five thousand lire note*

• **da** + **molto** (= 'a lot'), **poco** (= 'not much'), **troppo** (= 'too much'), **niente** (= 'nothing'), **nulla** (= 'nothing'), **qualcosa** (= 'something') and **tanto** (= 'so much') + infinitive = 'to':

Ho molto **da** fare.	*I have a lot to do.*
C'è qualcosa **da** bere?	*Is there something (anything) to drink?*

Da is also used to mean 'for' with periods of time (see page 95).

▼ *di* = 'of'

Di usually becomes **d'** before a vowel. Here is a list of its most common uses:

una tazza **di caffè**	*a cup of coffee*
una partita **di calcio**	*a football match*
un vestito **di lana**	*a woollen dress*
un'opera **di Verdi**	*an opera by Verdi*
Noi siamo **di Londra**.	*We are from London.*
alle dieci **di mattina**	*at ten in the morning*

• **di** is very often used with a verb before the infinitive of another verb (see page 79):

Ho dimenticato **di andare** alla banca. *I forgot to go to the bank.*

- **di** is also used with some adjectives before an infinitive:

Lieto di conoscerLa.   *Pleased to meet you.*
Sono **ansioso di** vederli.   *I am anxious to see them.*

- Some other prepositions are always used with **di** when they are followed by a noun:

fuori di = 'outside (of)'
fuori della casa   *outside the house*

but if you drop the definite article you do not use **di** and the meaning becomes wider than simply 'outside':

fuori casa   *away from home*
fuori città   *out of town*
fuori gioco   *offside*

prima di = 'before'
l'ultimo negozio prima dell'incrocio   *the last shop before the crossroads*
prima di mezzogiorno   *before midday*

- For the use of a preposition + **di** before an emphatic pronoun, see page 64.

▼ *dietro = 'behind'*

dietro la casa   *behind the house*
dietro l'angolo   *round the corner*

▼ *dopo = 'after'*

dopo le due   *after two o'clock*
dopo il semaforo   *after the traffic lights*

▼ *fra, tra = 'among', 'between'*
There is no difference between **fra** and **tra** and you can usually use either:

fra (tra) amici   *among friends*
L'albergo si trova **fra** (tra) piazza Garibaldi e via Roma.   *The hotel is (to be found) between piazza Garibaldi and via Roma.*

È **fra** i migliori della città.   *It's among the best in the city.*

- **fra/tra** + expression of time is used to translate 'in' or 'after':

Il treno parte **tra** (fra) un'ora.　　*The train leaves in an hour.*

▼ *in* = 'in', 'into'

L'ho trovato **in** un negozio di via Mazzini.　　*I found it in a shop on via Mazzini.*
L'ho messo **in** una busta.　　*I put it into an envelope.*
Andiamo **in** città　　*Let's go into town.*

- **in** + name of country

Andiamo in Italia.　　*We are going to Italy.*

- **in** + material is used to describe what something is made of (a bit more specific than **di**):

un armadio in legno　　*a wooden wardrobe*
una borsa in cuoio　　*a leather bag*

▼ *oltre* = 'beyond'

oltre il fiume　　*beyond the river*

▼ *per* = 'for', 'through'

Gli spaghetti sono **per** me.　　*The spaghetti is for me.*
Facciamo una passeggiata **per** il villaggio.　　*Let's take a walk through the village.*

▼ *senza* = 'without'

This is almost always used without the article:

Sono uscito **senza** ombrello.　　*I went out without an umbrella.*

▼ *sopra* = 'above', 'over'

una nebbia sopra la città　　*a fog over the city*

▼ *sotto* = 'under'

sotto il ponte　　*under the bridge*

▼ *su* = 'on'

Mettete i fiori **sulla** tavola.	*Put the flowers on the table.*
un articolo **su** Venezia	*an article on (about) Venice*

- **su** can also have the sense of 'up':

lassù **sulla** montagna	*up there on the mountain*
Andiamo **su**?	*Shall we go up?*

Note also:

Su, andiamo!	*Come on, let's go!*

▼ *verso* = 'towards', 'around'

verso Torino	*towards Turin*
verso sera	*towards (getting on for) evening*
verso le cinque	*around five o'clock*

▼ Prepositions used with verbs

When you have a first verb followed by another verb in the infinitive, sometimes you need a preposition between the two verbs. The two prepositions which can be used in this way in Italian are **a** and **di**. However, in some cases there is no need for a preposition between the main verb and the infinitive.

   You should learn the most common structures, as given in the lists below.

▼ *Common verbs followed by the infinitive with no preposition*

amare = *to love to*
bastare = *to suffice* (impersonal)
bisognare = *to need* (impersonal)
desiderare = *to want to*
dovere = *to have to*
fare = *to make (something happen)*
lasciare = *to allow to*
occorrere = *to be necessary* (impersonal)
osare = *to dare to*
parere = *to seem to*
piacere = *to please*

potere = *to be able to*
preferire = *to prefer to*
sapere = *to know how to*
sembrare = *to seem to*
sentire = *to hear (something happening)*
vedere = *to see (something happening)*
volere = *to want to*

Preferisco restare qui.	*I prefer to stay here.*
L'ho visto passare pochi minuti fa.	*I saw him go by a few minutes ago.*
Basta firmare qui.	*It is enough to sign here.*

▼ *Common verbs followed by 'a' + the infinitive*

affrettarsi a = *to hurry to*
aiutare a = *to help to*
andare a = *to go to (do something)*
cominciare a = *to begin to*
continuare a = *to continue to*
correre a = *to run to (do something)*
costringere a = *to compel to*
decidersi a = *to make up one's mind to*
dedicarsi a = *to devote oneself to*
divertirsi a = *to enjoy oneself (doing something)*
imparare a = *to learn to*
incoraggiare a = *to encourage to*
insegnare a = *to teach to*
invitare a = *to invite to (do something)*
mandare a = *to send to (do something)*
mettersi a = *to begin to*
pensare a = *to think of (doing something)*
persuadere a = *to persuade to*
preparare a = *to prepare to*
provare a = *to try to*
riprendere a = *to resume (doing something)*
riuscire a = *to succeed in, to manage to*
servire a = *to be good for*
stare a = *to stay, stand (doing something)*
tornare a = *to return to (doing something)*
venire a = *to come to (do something)*

Penso a scriverti.	*I am thinking of writing to you.*
Cominciò a ridere.	*He started to laugh.*
Sono venuta a trovarti.	*I have come to see you.*
È riuscito a farlo.	*He managed to do it.*

▼ *Common verbs followed by 'di' + the infinitive*

The following verbs take **di** when followed by an infinitive, but **che** + subjunctive (see pages 122–131) with another clause:

accettare di = *to accept (doing)*
accorgersi di = *to notice (doing)*
ammettere di = *to admit to*
aspettare di = *to wait to*
aspettarsi di = *to expect to*
avere bisogno di = *to need to*
avere fretta di = *to be in a hurry to*
avere il tempo di = *to have the time to*
avere l'impressione di = *to have the feeling of (doing)*
avere intenzione di = *to intend to*
avere paura di = *to fear to*
avere vergogna di = *to be ashamed to*
avere voglia di = *to feel like*
cercare di = *to try to*
cessare di = *to cease (doing)*
chiedere di = *to ask to*
comandare di = *to order to*
consigliare di = *to advise to*
credere di = *to believe (that one is doing something)*
decidere di = *to decide to*
dimenticare di = *to forget to*
dire di = *to tell to*
domandare di = *to ask to*
dubitare di = *to doubt (that one is doing something)*
fare a meno di = *to do without (doing something)*
fingere di = *to pretend to*
finire di = *to finish (doing something)*
impedire di = *to prevent (doing something)*
minacciare di = *to threaten to*
offrire di = *to offer to*
pensare di = *to plan to*
pentirsi di = *to repent (doing something)*
permettere di = *to allow (to do something)*
pregare di = *to beg to*

promettere di = *to promise to*
proporre di = *to propose to*
rendersi conto di = *to realise*
ricordarsi di = *to remember to*
rifiutarsi di = *to refuse to*
sapere di = *to know*
smettere di = *to stop*
sognare di = *to dream (about doing something)*
sperare di = *to hope to*
stancarsi di = *to get tired of (doing something)*
suggerire di = *to suggest (doing something)*
tentare di = *to try to*
vergognarsi di = *to be ashamed of (doing something)*
vietare di = *to forbid to*

Non ammette di aver torto.	*He doesn't admit being wrong.*
Non ho voglia di mangiare.	*I don't feel like eating.*
Ho dimenticato di dirti.	*I forgot to tell you.*

▼ *Common verbs followed by 'a' + person + 'di' + the infinitive*

Some verbs can be followed by both **a** followed by a person and **di** followed by an infinitive:

chiedere a (qualcuno) di (fare qualcosa) = *to ask (someone) to (do something)*
comandare a .... di .... = *to order to*
consigliare a .... di .... = *to advise to*
dire a .... di .... = *to ask, tell to*
domandare a .... di .... = *to ask to*
impedire a .... di .... = *to forbid to*
ordinare a .... di .... = *to order to*
permettere a .... di .... = *to permit to*
proibire a .... di .... = *to forbid to*
promettere a .... di .... = *to promise to*
proporre a .... di .... = *to propose to*
ricordare a .... di .... = *to remind to*
suggerire a .... di .... = *to suggest that*
vietare a .... di .... = *to forbid to*

Consiglio a mia mamma di riposarsi.	*I advise my mother to rest.*
Abbiamo chiesto al tassista di aspettare.	*We asked the taxi driver to wait.*

▼ *Common verbs followed by 'su'*

contare su = *to count on*
giurare su = *to swear on*
riflettere su = *to think about*
scommettere su = *to bet on*

Puoi contare su di me.   *You can count on me.*
Abbiamo riflettuto sugli argomenti. *We have thought about the questions.*
Ho scommesso molto su quel cavallo. *I have bet a lot on that horse.*

▼ Activity 1   *Prepositions*

Use suitable prepositions or phrases for the words in brackets to complete the following.

a Vieni (with me) (to the) parrucchiere. Il negozio è (in front of the) albergo.

b Questa è la strada che va (towards) Siena. Viene (from) Bologna e passa (through) Firenze.

c Andiamo (into town). Prendiamo il tram (as far as the) piazza. Possiamo mangiare (in the) trattoria (beside the) duomo.

d La mensa (of the) studenti è (round the corner) (on the right).

e Cerco (to) finire, ma (I have too much to do).

VERBS
identifying what is happening

The verb is the engine of a language. It is the word (or combination of words) that drives the meaning. You might freewheel a little without a verb in the Tarzan manner ('me Tarzan, you Jane, he Boy'), but as soon as you want to get anywhere you need to use a verb ('Tarzan swim, Boy play, Jane work'). And if you tune it properly, with the right endings (unlike Tarzan), the sentence will run smoothly and the meaning will be clear.

Verbs are often called 'doing' words. Most of the time that is true enough, but some verbs do not 'do' anything – they just 'are'. And there is one part of a verb which just 'ticks over' without sparking into action. It is known as the **infinitive**.

▼ The infinitive

The infinitive is almost like the 'name' of the verb. It gives the general idea of the verb without saying anything about who, what or when. We recognise it in English because it uses the word 'to' ('to buy', 'to sell', 'to sleep', etc.). In Italian, you recognise the infinitive of the verb from the endings '-are', '-ere', and '-ire':

comprare = *to buy*   vendere = *to sell*
dormire = *to sleep*

All Italian verbs fall into one of these three groups (or **conjugations**, as they are often called). You should think of each as having an **identity vowel** – 'a' for the first (-**are**) group, 'e' for the second (-**ere**) group, and 'i' for the third (-**ire**) group. This will often help you with the endings for different tenses.

There are a few verbs whose infinitive ends in '-rre', e.g. **condurre** (= 'to lead'), **ridurre** (= 'to reduce'), **porre** (= 'to put'), **trarre** (= 'to bring, drag'). These work like verbs ending in '-**ere**' because they come from an original (and now lost) form; for example, **condurre** comes from **conducere**, and the 'stem' is **conduc-**.

Other verbs whose infinitives were originally in an extended form are **fare** (= 'to do, make') from **facere**, which apart from the present tense works like an '-**ere**' verb; **dire** (= 'to say') from **dicere**, so the stem is **dic-**; **bere** (= 'to drink') from **bevere**, so the stem is **bev-**.

▼ Tenses: the 'when' of the verb

When we say 'I buy' (or 'I am buying'), we are obviously talking about something that is happening in the present. When we say 'I bought' (or 'I have bought'), we are talking about what we did in the past. And when we say 'I will buy', we are thinking into the future. Present, past and future are **tenses** of the verb. 'Tense' means 'time'. (Think of a bad pronunciation of the French word **temps**, which is where the words 'tense' comes from.)

The form of the verb itself tells us when something takes place, even without additional information such as 'today', 'tomorrow' or 'last year'. In English, the verb sometimes has the same form as the infinitive ('I buy'); sometimes we add another verb and/or change the ending ('I will buy', 'I am buying'); and sometimes we change the word completely ('I bought').

In Italian, too, the 'when' is shown in the verb itself. The present tense is usually shown by the endings. The most common way to indicate the past is to add another verb (similar to the English 'I have bought'), while for the future it is again the endings that change.

▼ Making the verb agree with its subject

In Italian, the ending of the verb also always tells you who (or 'what' if it is not a person) is the subject of the verb, i.e. the one carrying out the action or in charge of the verb. Because of this, you seldom need to use the subject pronoun (see pages 54–55).

If you cut off the infinitive endings, you are left with the **stem** of the verb (**compr-**, **vend-**, **dorm-**), on to which you add the appropriate person and tense endings.

Most verbs follow a regular pattern of endings and so are known as **regular** verbs. Those that have some differences are known as **irregular** verbs, but even with these there is a recognisable system to the endings.

▼ Questions

To form a question in Italian, all you have to do is raise the tone of your voice when speaking, or put a question mark at the end when writing:

Vende i surgelati?	*Do you sell frozen food?*
Il film finisce tardi?	*Does the film finish late?*
Vieni con noi?	*Are you coming with us?*

You can also put the subject **after** the verb (but you do not separate the verb from the adverb):

Finisce tardi il film?	*Does the film finish late?*
Vengono con noi i ragazzi?	*Are the boys coming with us?*

But:
When you use question words such as **quando** (= 'when?'), **a che ora** (= 'when?', 'at what time?'), **dove** (= 'where?'), **perchè** (= 'why?'), **cosa** (or **che**, or **che cosa**) (= 'what?'), then you **must** put the subject after the verb:

Quando (a che ora) finisce il film?	*When does the film finish?*
Dove sono i ragazzi?	*Where are the boys?*
Perchè compra la signora tutta quella roba?	*Why is the lady buying all that stuff?*
Cosa ti compra tuo marito per il compleanno?	*What is your husband buying you for your birthday?*
Che cosa vogliono fare quei signori?	*What do those men want to do?*

▼ *Question tags*
In English, we often use phrases such as 'isn't it?', 'don't you?' etc. at the end of a sentence. The equivalent in Italian is **vero?** or **non è vero?**:

Il gelato è buono, **vero**?	*The ice-cream is good, isn't it?*
Sì (è vero).	*Yes (it is).*
Lei sa dove andiamo, **non è vero**?	*You know where we are going, don't you? No (I don't).*
No (non è vero).	

▼ Negatives

To say something in the negative, all you have to do is put **non** in front of the verb:

Il film **non** finisce tardi.	*The film doesn't finish late.*

If there is an object pronoun with the verb, you put the **non** in front of it:

La signora **non la** compra per se stessa.	*The lady isn't buying it for herself.*

Italian uses the double negative:

Non vedo **nessuno**.	*I don't see anyone.*
Non dico **niente**.	*I am not saying anything.*
Non è **nè** pesce **nè** carne.	*It is neither fish nor fowl.*

▼ Impersonal verbs

Some verbs are only ever used in the third person (the equivalent of 'it'), because the action is not done by people:

piovere = *to rain*	piove = *it's raining*
nevicare = *to snow*	nevica = *it's snowing*
accadere = *to happen*	accade spesso = *it happens often*
succedere = *to happen*	succede così = *it happens like this*

There are several ways to say 'it is necessary' using impersonal verbs:

Bisogna andare subito.	*It is necessary/We need to go at once.*

Occorre andare subito.
Ci tocca andare subito.

■ To like and to need

Italian expresses this differently from English. Instead of saying, 'I like it', you have to say, 'it is pleasing to me'. The verb for 'to please' is **piacere**. It is used with the indirect object personal pronoun (**mi, ti, gli, le, ci, vi, gli, loro**) or with **a** + noun. It is practically only ever used in the third person singular and plural (unless you want to ask **ti piaccio?** = 'do you like me?'):

Mi piace quella musica.	*I like that music.*
Bambini, **vi piacciono** le caramelle?	*Do you like sweets, children?*
Il governo attuale **non piace** alle banche.	*The banks do not like the present government.*
Mi piace viaggiare.	*I like travelling (to travel).*

Note that here the infinitive **viaggiare** acts like a singular noun and is the subject of **piace**.

It is possible to use the verb **amare** (= 'to love') instead, but it is often too strong for 'like'.

The same kind of construction is used occasionally for 'to need', with the verbs **occorrere** and **servire**:

Mi occorrono degli spilli.	*I need some pins.*
Mi servono degli spiccioli per il telefono.	*I need some small change for the telephone.*

Il piacere is the noun meaning 'pleasure'. The standard response to being introduced to someone is

Piacere di conoscerLa.	*Pleased to meet you, make your acquaintance.*

▼ The present tense

We have three ways of expressing the present tense in English: 'I buy', 'I am buying', 'I do buy'. ('I do buy' is more often used in the negative – 'I do not buy' – and in the question form – 'do I buy?') Italian has one form for the three English meanings. (There is another one for the 'am buying' meaning which we shall see later.) So **vendiamo** means 'we sell' or 'we are selling' or 'we do sell':

Non **vendiamo** i surgelati, ma **vendiamo** la carne fresca. Oggi **vendiamo** agnello di stagione.	*We do not sell frozen food, but we do sell fresh meat. Today we are selling this season's lamb.*

The tables below show the pattern for the present tenses of regular verbs and the most commonly-used irregular verbs.

▼ *Forming the present tense – regular verbs*
Note: verbs of the third (**-ire**) group can be subdivided into those where '**-isc-**' is added to the stem of the present tense, except in the **noi** and **voi** forms (e.g. **finire** = 'to finish'), and those where it is not (e.g. **dormire** = 'to sleep'). Apart from that, they follow identical patterns. There is no way of telling which is which other than by listening, learning and remembering.

	Group 1 -are	Group 2 -ere	Group 3a -ire	Group 3b -ire
	comprare *to buy*	vendere *to sell*	dormire *to sleep*	finire *to finish*
io	compro	vendo	dormo	finisco
tu	compri	vendi	dormi	finisci
lui lei Lei	compra	vende	dorme	finisce
noi	compriamo	vendiamo	dormiamo	finiamo
voi	comprate	vendete	dormite	finite
loro	comprano	vendono	dormono	finiscono

As you can see, the endings vary little between the groups. It is best to try to memorise the verbs without the pronouns, as this creates a more natural rhythm.

Note the following points on pronunciation:

- Most second group (-**ere**) verbs have an unstressed ending on the infinitive, as in v**e**ndere, but some have a stress on the first 'e' of the ending, as in ved**e**re (= 'to see'). It makes no difference to the endings or pronunciation of the rest of the verb parts, which all follow the regular second group pattern.

- The stress on the third person plural form (the **loro** form) is always away from the ending, on the third-last syllable.

▼ *Spelling and pronunciation changes*

Spelling changes are often necessary to keep the sound of the verb consistent when the endings change. for example:

- Verbs ending in '-**iare**' have only one 'i' in the ending of the **tu** form:

mangiare = 'to eat'
mangio, mangi, mangia, mangiamo, mangiate, mangiano

cominciare = 'to begin'
comincio, cominci, comincia, cominciamo, cominciate, cominciano

Common exception

inviare = 'to send'
invio, invii, invia, inviamo, inviate, inviano

- Verbs ending in '-**care**' or '-**gare**' need an 'h' before a soft vowel to keep the hard 'k' or 'g' sound:

cercare = 'to look for'
cerco, cer**ch**i, cerca, cer**ch**iamo, cercate, cercano

pagare = 'to pay'
pago, pa**gh**i, paga, pa**gh**iamo, pagate, pagano

- Verbs ending in '-**scere**', '-**cere**' and '-**gere**' do not change the spelling, so the pronunciation changes to a hard 'k' or 'g' in front of 'o' in the ending:

conoscere = 'to know'
cono**sco**, conosci, conosce, conosciamo, conoscete, cono**sco**no

crescere = 'to grow'
cre**sco**, cresci, cresce, cresciamo, crescete, cre**sco**no

leggere = 'to read'
le**gg**o, leggi, legge, leggiamo, leggete, le**gg**ono

- Some verbs ending in '-**gliere**' change spelling and pronunciation in the **io** and **loro** forms:

acc**o**gliere = 'to welcome, receive'
acc**olg**o, accogli, accoglie, accogliamo, accogliete, acc**olg**ono

- Some verbs ending in '-**ggire**' do not change the spelling in the **io** and **loro** forms, and so the pronunciation changes to the hard 'g' sound in front of 'o':

fuggire = 'to flee' (also **sfug**gire = 'to escape')
fu**gg**o, fuggi, fugge, fuggiamo, fuggite, fu**gg**ono

▼ Activity 1   *The present tense*

Write out the full present tense of the following verbs:

Group 1 -are

aiutare (= *to help*)	giocare (= *to play*)
cambiare (= *to change*)	guardare (= *to look at*)
ascoltare (= *to listen (to)*)	arrivare (= *to arrive*)
lavorare (= *to work*)	parlare (= *to speak*)
entrare (= *to enter*)	studiare (= *to study*)

Group 2 -ere

vedere (= *to see*)	prendere (= *to take*)
cadere (= *to fall*)	chiudere (= *to close*)
mettere (= *to put*)	ricevere (= *to receive*)
scendere (= *to go down, get off*)	scrivere (= *to write*)
ripetere (= *to repeat*)	spendere (= *to spend*)

Group 3a -ire

aprire (= *to open*)	coprire (= *to cover*)
offrire (= *to offer*)	soffrire (= *to suffer*)
servire (= *to serve*)	seguire (= *to follow*)

Group 3b -ire

capire (= *to understand*)	pulire (= *to clean*)
preferire (= *to prefer*)	suggerire (= *to suggest*)
costruire (= *to build*)	guarire (= *to heal*)

▼ *Forming the present tense – common irregular verbs*
The two most commonly-used verbs are:

essere = *to be*   avere = *to have*

You need them all the time, not only to say 'be' and 'have' but also because they are used to make up the ordinary past tenses (see pages 99–101). These are the present tenses. It is worth memorising them straight away.

	essere	avere
io	sono	ho
tu	sei	hai
lui		
lei	è	ha
Lei		
noi	siamo	abbiamo
voi	siete	avete
loro	sono	hanno

■ **Shortened forms**
It is very common for forms to be shortened, so that instead of **sono qui** (= 'I am here') you will often hear **son qui**. This can be done only when the shortened word ends with 'm', 'n', 'r', or 'l'. So you can never shorten **siete** or **avete**, for example, but you may hear **abbiam pagato** (= 'we have paid') instead of **abbiamo pagato**.

It is common for **avere** to be shortened to **aver**, but there is no rule that can be followed for this.

■ **Common expressions with 'avere'**

• **aver freddo** = 'to be cold'

• **aver caldo** = 'to be hot, warm'

Freddo and **caldo** are nouns, not adjectives, in these phrases, so they do not change endings.

➤

The expressions are only used of a person (or an animal) 'feeling' cold/hot:

ho caldo = *I am hot/warm*

il caffè è caldo = *the coffee is hot*

hanno molto freddo = *they are very cold   very unfriendly*

sono molto freddi = *they are very unfriendly*

- **aver ragione** = 'to be right'
- **aver torto** = 'to be wrong'
- **aver paura (di)** = 'to be afraid (of)'

Ho paura del buio.   *I'm afraid of the dark.*
Ho paura di andarci.   *I'm afraid to go there.*

- **aver fortuna** = 'to be lucky' (also **<u>e</u>ssere fortunato**)
- **aver sonno** = 'to be sleepy'
- **avere fretta** = 'to be in a hurry'
- **avere bisogno di** = 'to need' (have need of)

Ho bisogno di una nuova m<u>a</u>cchina.   *I need a new car.*
Ho bisogno di cambiare la m<u>a</u>cchina.   *I need to change my car.*

- **avere da + infinitive** = 'to have to'

Ho da cambiare la m<u>a</u>cchina.   *I have to change my car.*
Ho molto da fare.   *I have a lot to do.*

The two most common verbs expressing movement are:

	andare *to go*	**venire** *to come*
io	vado	vengo
tu	vai	vieni
lui **lei** **Lei**	va	viene
noi	andiamo	veniamo
voi	andate	venite
loro	vanno	v<u>e</u>ngono

Lui **va** a Firenze.   *He is going to Florence.*
Giulietta **viene** da Verona.   *Juliet comes from Verona.*

Note the following expressions using **andare**:

* **andare a** + infinitive means 'to be going to' in the sense of an intention:

Vado a scrivergli domani.   *I'm going to write to him*
                                               tomorrow.

* **andarsene** = 'to go away':

me ne vado = *I'm going away, I'm off!*

* **andare via** is an alternative for 'to go away' – **via** never changes. **Via!** is often used on its own meaning 'shoo!' or 'go!' (as in a race).

Note: a few other verbs have a stem that changes in the present tense in the same way as **venire**. There is no rule, but they are easily remembered:

* **tenere** = 'to hold'

tengo, tieni, tiene, teniamo, tenete, tengono

* **sedersi** = 'to sit down'

mi siedo (seggo), ti siedi, si siede, ci sediamo, vi sedete, si siedono (seggono)

▼ *Other irregular verbs in common everyday use*

* **fare** = 'to do, make'

faccio, fai, fa, facciamo, fate, fanno

L'idraulico **fa** molto disturbo, ma   *The plumber causes a lot of*
fa un buon lavoro.   *disturbance, but he does a good*
                                               job.

Fare + infinitive means 'to have something done':

Faccio riparare il rubinetto.   *I'm having the tap repaired.*
Mi **faccio fare** un vestito nuovo.   *I'm having a new suit made for*
                                               myself.

■ **Common expressions with 'fare'**

Fare is used:

• with expressions of weather:

fa freddo = *it is cold*
fa caldo = *it is hot* } (only of weather)
fa brutto tempo = *it is filthy weather*

• to express hurt, pain, pleasure, etc.:

Mi **fanno male** i piedi.	*My feet hurt.*
Ci **fa piacere** rivedervi.	*We are pleased to see you again.*
Un pò di vino **fa bene**.	*A little wine is good for you.*

Note also:

fa lo stesso = *it's all the same, it comes to the same thing*
(non) fa niente = *it doesn't matter*

• **potere = 'to be able, (can)'**

posso, puoi, può, possiamo, potete, p<u>o</u>ssono

Most of the time, **potere** is followed by the infinitive:

Vieni stasera? No, **non posso venire**.	*Are you coming tonight? No, I can't come.*
Il bambino **non può fare** questo compito perchè e troppo diff<u>i</u>cile.	*The child is not able to do this homework (task) because it is too difficult.*

but it is occasionally used alone:

posso? = *may I?*	prego = *please do, certainly*

• **sapere = 'to know'**

so, sai, sa, sappiamo, sapete, sanno

Note: **sapere** means to know in the case of facts; **conoscere** means to know in the sense of being acquainted with:

Conosco un buon parrucchiere ma non **so** se lavora oggi.	*I know a good hairdresser but I don't know if he's working today.*

Sapere + infinitive also means 'to be able ('can') in the sense of 'to know how to do something':

Non **sanno** parlare inglese.	*They can't speak English.*
Il bambino **sa** già leggere.	*The child can already read.*
E **sa** anche nuotare.	*And he can also swim.*

- **volere** = 'to want'

voglio, vuoi, vuole, vogliamo, volete, vogliono

Volere + infinitive = 'to want to':

Voglio un biglietto per la lotteria perchè **voglio vincere** tanti soldi.	*I want a ticket for the lottery because I want to win lots of money.*

Note the common expression **voler dire** = 'to mean':

Cosa **vuol dire** questa parola?	*What does this word mean?*

- **dovere** = 'to have to (must)'

devo (debbo), devi, deve, dobbiamo, dovete, devono (debbono)

It is followed by the infinitive:

Dobbiamo fare un appuntamento con la parrucchiera per domani.	*We must make an appointment with the hairdresser for tomorrow.*

It can also mean 'must' implying probability:

Il negozio **deve essere** qui vicino.	*The shop must be near here.*

When it is followed by a direct object, **dovere** means 'to owe':

Lui **deve** pagare perchè **deve** cinquantamila lire.	*He has to pay because he owes fifty thousand lire.*

Note: see the Verb Tables on pages 147–154 for the present tenses of other irregular verbs.

▼ Activity 2 *Questions and negatives in the present*

Translate into Italian:

- Why do you not want to come tomorrow? Don't you like the countryside (la campagna)?
- I have to go to buy a present (un regalo) for my husband. Do you know a shop where they sell nice ties?
- I don't know where the best shops are.
- We can ask (chi<u>e</u>dere) in the hotel. They know everything.

▼ *Other uses of the present tense*

• The present tense is very often used to refer to something in the future, just as it is in English:

P<u>a</u>rtono domani.	*They are leaving tomorrow.*
L'anno pr<u>o</u>ssimo **andiamo** in Am<u>e</u>rica.	*Next year we are going to America.*

• It is also used to describe something that started in the past and is still going on, using the preposition **da**:

Sono qui da anni.	*I've been here for years.*
Lui **lavora** qui da tre mesi.	*He has been working here for three months.*
Non **piove** da maggio.	*It hasn't rained since May.*

• It is also used for something in the very immediate future where in English we would say 'I'll' or 'I will', etc.:

Adesso ti **compro** un gelato.	*Now I'll buy you an ice-cream.*
Mangiamo dopo?	*Shall we eat afterwards?*

▼ *The present continuous tense*
In addition to the verb <u>e</u>ssere there is another verb meaning 'to be':

Stare = 'to be', 'to stay'

sto, stai, sta, stiamo, state, stanno

- It is mainly used with expressions of health (see page 52):

sto bene = *I am well*   sto male = *I am ill*

- It is also sometimes used when talking about location, particularly in southern Italy:

Dove sta il municipio?   *Where is the town hall?*

- It is used in the physical sense of 'to stay' (not the residential sense, which is **abitare** = 'to reside', or the sense of remaining, which is **rimanere** or **restare**):

Io **sto** qui e non mi muovo.   *I'm staying here and I'll not move.*
Sta sempre in piedi.   *He's still standing (staying on his feet).*

- It is also used to mean 'to suit' or 'to go with':

Ti stanno bene i capelli lunghi.   *Long hair suits you.*
La cravatta a righe sta bene   *The striped tie goes well with the*
con la giacca sportiva.   *sports jacket.*

- **stare per** + infinitive means 'to be about to', 'to be on the point of':

Il negozio sta per chiudere.   *The shop is about to close.*

Stare is also used to form the equivalent of the English continuous present ('I am going', etc.) It is used together with the **present participle**.

The present participle is the equivalent of the English ending '-ing'. It is formed by taking the stem of the verb and adding '-**ando**' for '-**are**' verbs, or '-**endo**' for '-**ere**' and '-**ire**' verbs:

parlando = *speaking*   leggendo = *reading*
aprendo = *opening*

Present participles are regular, e.g. **essendo** from **essere**, **avendo** from **avere**, but there are a few which are irregular: **facendo** from **fare**, **dicendo** from **dire** (= 'to say'). This is because their infinitives are really shortened forms of the original 'facere' and 'dicere' (see page 83).

Other verbs like this which you will need are **bevendo** from **bere** (= 'to drink') and **conducendo** from **condurre** (= 'to lead').

The present continuous is used to underline the fact that the person is in the process of, or in the middle of, or busy doing the action. If you are not emphasising this idea, use the simple present tense, even if you would use the continuous in English.

Ti **sto parlando**.	*I am (in the middle of) speaking to you.*
Sta leggendo il giornale.	*He is (busy) reading the newspaper.*
Stanno aprendo le porte.	*They are (in the process of) opening the doors.*
Di che cosa **sta parlando** quel signore?	*What is that gentleman talking about?*

▼ Activity 3   *Present and present continuous*

Translate the following sentences into Italian using the appropriate tense for each verb.

a I can't come just now. I'm writing a letter to my mother.
b What does that man want? He's calling us.
c Where does this bus go to? I want to go to via Manzoni.
d Do you know Milan well? I have to be at my hotel at five o'clock.
e I like travelling by bus (in <u>a</u>utobus) because I can see the whole city.

▼ The perfect tense

The perfect tense is the equivalent of the English 'I have bought', etc. In Italian it is now also used for the simple past tense (the equivalent of English 'I bought'). As in English, it is made up of two verbs: the first one shows who did the action and the second what was done. In English, the first verb (the **auxiliary**, since it helps out) is always the present tense of the verb 'to have'. In Italian, the auxiliary verb is the present tense of either **avere** or **essere**. The second (main) verb is always in the form of the **past participle**.

▼ *The past participle*

Just as you can recognise the present participle from the ending '-ndo', so you can easily recognise the past participle from the ending '-to' (or, in the case of a lot of irregular verbs, '-so'). The regular past participles are:

• -are verbs: -ato

comprato

• -ere verbs: -uto

venduto

• -ire verbs: -ito

dormito, finito

Past participles of other verbs:

essere – **stato**	stare – **stato**
avere – **avuto**	sapere – **saputo**
volere – **voluto**	dovere – **dovuto**
venire – **venuto**	potere – **potuto**
fare – **fatto**	dire – **detto**

Remember to insert an 'i' into verbs ending in '-scere' to keep the sound:

conoscere – **conosciuto**	crescere – **cresciuto**

Irregular past participles of other common verbs:

leggere – **letto**	scrivere – **scritto**
vedere – **visto** (sometimes also **veduto**)	
perdere – **perso** (sometimes also **perduto**)	
accogliere – **accolto**	condurre – **condotto**
prendere – **preso**	mettere – **messo**
chiudere – **chiuso**	scendere – **sceso**
spendere – **speso**	chiedere – **chiesto**
aprire – **aperto**	coprire – **coperto**
offrire – **offerto**	scoprire – **scoperto**

(See also the Verb Tables, pages 147–154.)

▼ *Forming the perfect tense using 'avere'*

The present tense of **avere** is used as the auxiliary verb in the perfect tense with:

- main verbs which take a direct object (**transitive** verbs). You can tell if a verb takes a direct object if you can ask the question 'what?':

Ha avuto un infarto.   *He had (has had) a heart attack.*

(*question*: he had what? *answer*: a heart attack – **direct object**)

Ho saputo che **ha avuto** un infarto.   *I knew (got to know) that he had a heart attack.*

(*question*: I knew what? *answer*: <u>that he had a heart attack</u> – the whole underlined phrase is the direct object)

- some main verbs which do not take a direct object (**intransitive** verbs), but which express some kinds of action or state (physical or mental), e.g. **parlare** (= 'to speak'), **cenare** (= 'to have supper, dine'), **dormire**, **camminare** (= 'to walk'), **viaggiare** (= 'to travel'), **sorridere** (= 'to smile').

Abbiamo sorriso quando **ha parlato** lui, perchè non **ha detto** la verità.   *We smiled when he spoke because he did not tell the truth.*

▼ Activity 4   *Perfect tense*

Change the following into the perfect tense using 'avere':

a   compro
b   dormiamo
c   prendono
d   vogliamo
e   potete
f   vendi
g   finisco
h   dico
i   sanno
j   apre

▼ *Agreement of the past participle when using 'avere'*
When you are using **avere** in the perfect tense, the past
participle usually stays in the masculine singular form:

Le **ho detto** che abbiamo visto molte cose.	*I told her that we have seen a lot of things.*

But:
When one of the direct object pronouns **lo**, **la**, **li** and **le** is
used, the past participle agrees with it in number and gender:

La cena **l'ha pagata** lui.	*He paid for the dinner.*
Dove sono i giornali? **Li** avete **buttati**? Non **li** ho ancora **letti**.	*Where are the newspapers? Have you thrown them away? I haven't read them yet.*

Note the following points:

• When the direct object pronoun is **La** (the polite form of
'you'), the agreement of the past participle depends on
whether La (you) refers to a male or a female:

L'ho visto ieri, signore.	*I saw you yesterday, sir.*

• When the direct object pronoun is **mi**, **ti**, **ci** or **vi**, the past
participle may or may not agree. There is no rule to follow:
it is a matter of personal preference.

Rosanna, ti ho **invitata** (ti ho invitato).	*Rosanna, I have invited you.*

• Nowadays, there is no agreement with **che** as a preceding
direct object:

Ecco i biglietti che abbiamo comprato.	*Here are the tickets that we have bought.*

but you may well see **comprati** in more formal kinds of writing.

▼ Activity 5 — *Agreement with preceding direct object*

The past participles in these sentences are underlined. Make them agree with the preceding direct object where appropriate.

a Vedi quella signora? L'ho <u>incontrato</u> ieri.
b Le abbiamo <u>dato</u> i regali che abbiamo <u>comprato</u>.
c Non trovo più le chiavi. Penso che le ho <u>perso</u>.
d Vi abbiamo <u>visto</u> ieri sera al concerto.
e Buongiorno, signora Viggiani. L'ho <u>chiamato</u> per telefono ma non L'ho <u>trovato</u> a casa.

▼ *Forming the perfect tense using 'essere'*

The present tense of **essere** is used as the auxiliary verb in the perfect tense with:

• most intransitive verbs, especially those which express movement:

essere = *to be*	salire = *to go up*
andare = *to go*	partire = *to leave, set off*
venire = *to come*	rimanere (rimasto) = *to remain*
cadere = *to fall*	sembrare = *to seem*
arrivare = *to arrive*	piacere = *to please*
scendere = *to go down*	

Siete stati a vedere il duomo?	*Have you been to see the cathedral?*
La Torre Pendente di Pisa non è ancora **caduta**.	*The Leaning Tower of Pisa has not yet fallen down.*
Siamo saliti sul tram e poi **siamo scesi** in piazza Oberdan.	*We got on (up into) the tram and then we got off (got down) in piazza Oberdan.*

• sembrare and piacere:

Mi è **sembrato** giusto insistere.	*I thought it right to insist.*
Mi è **piaciuta** la trattoria dove abbiamo mangiato ieri sera.	*I liked the trattoria where we ate last night.*

- Reflexive verbs (those which use reflexive pronouns – see pages 61–63), where the subject and object of the verb are the same. We do not always use the pronoun '-self' with the equivalent verbs in English, but it must be used in Italian:

lavarsi = *to wash (oneself)*
mi sono lavato = *I washed (or have washed) myself*

but

ho lavato i piatti = *I (have) washed the dishes*

(here the subject is different from the object so the verb takes **avere**)

alzarsi = *to get (oneself) up*
ci siamo alzati alle sette = *we got up at seven*

- reciprocal verbs (those using reciprocal pronouns – see page 62), where the subject and indirect object of the verb are the same:

Ci siamo dati un appuntamento alle sette.   *We made a date for seven o'clock.*

▼ *Agreement of the past participle when using 'essere'*
When you are using <u>essere</u> in the perfect tense, the past participle acts like an adjective – it always agrees in gender and number with the subject of the verb.

▼ *Use of 'avere' and 'essere' with 'potuto', dovuto' and 'voluto'*
When the perfect tense of **potere**, **dovere** or **volere** is followed by the infinitive of a verb that takes <u>essere</u> in the perfect tense, you may use either **avere** or <u>essere</u>:

Non siamo potuti andare.   ⎫
Non abbiamo potuto andare. ⎬ *We couldn't go.*
                            ⎭

When the perfect tense of **potere**, **dovere** or **volere** is followed by the infinitive of a reflexive verb, there are two alternatives:

- Use **avere** and attach the reflexive pronoun to the infinitive:

Ha dovuto alzarsi alle sette.   *He had to get up at seven.*
Ha voluto and<u>a</u>rsene.   *He wanted to go away.*

• Use <u>essere</u>, with the reflexive pronoun before the auxiliary verb:

Si è dovuto alzare alle sette.　*He had to get up at seven.*
Se n'è voluto andare.　*He wanted to go away.*

■ Transitive and intransitive

Some verbs are sometimes transitive (take an object) and sometimes intransitive (do not have an object). When they are transitive, the perfect tense is formed using **avere**:

Abbiamo finito la riunione alle sette.　*We finished the meeting at seven.*
Abbiamo corso la maratona di New York.　*We ran (we have run) the New York marathon.*

When they are used intransitively, the perfect tense is formed using <u>essere</u>:

La riunione **è finita** alle sette.　*The meeting finished at seven.*
Siamo corsi all'ospedale per vederti.　*We (have) rushed to the hospital to see you.*

▼ Activity 6　*Using 'avere' and 'essere'*

Put the words in brackets into the perfect tense. (The subject is also given where it might be unclear.)

a La settimana scorsa (noi andare) a vedere La Traviata alla Scala. Mi (piacere) molto.
b Tutti e tre (noi incontrarsi) davanti all'ingresso principale.
c (Noi entrare) e (salire) alla prima galleria.
d L'opera (cominciare) alle otto ed (finire) a mezzanotte.
e Quando (noi uscire), (correre) per prendere l'ultimo tram.

▼ The passive

Most of the time we use verbs in the **active** sense – that is when the subject 'acts upon' the object. In 'Claudio Abbado conducts the orchestra', the subject, 'Claudio Abbado', performs the action on the object, 'the orchestra', through the active form of the verb, 'conducts'. Looking at it from the orchestra's point of view, you could say, 'the orchestra is conducted by Claudio Abbado'. Put this way, the orchestra is the subject, but it is not 'doing' anything: it is being acted upon, it is **passive**. 'The orchestra is playing' is active; 'the orchestra is conducted' is passive.

▼ *Forming the passive*

In the same way as in English we use the verb 'to be' + past participle to make the passive ('is conducted'), so Italian uses the verb **essere** + past participle:

Claudio Abbado **dirige** l'orchestra.	*Claudio Abbado conducts the orchestra. (active)*
L'orchestra **è diretta** da Claudio Abbado.	*The orchestra is conducted by Claudio Abbado. (passive)*

The past participle always agrees in gender and number with the subject in passive constructions. (It acts as an adjective.)

Note: when using the passive, **da** is always used to translate 'by'.

For the perfect tense of a passive verb, use the perfect tense of **essere** instead of the present. Both past participles agree with the subject:

Siamo stati accompagnati da una guida eccellente.	*We were accompanied by an excellent guide.*

Sometimes, verbs other than **essere** are used to form the passive, to make slight changes in the meaning:

- **venire** is often used instead of **essere** to give the idea of the present continuous:

Il programma **viene trasmesso** sul Canale 5.	*The programme is being broadcast on Channel 5.*

or to give the idea of a repeated action:

Le partite **vengono giocate** la domenica.	*The matches are played on Sundays.*

- **andare** is often used instead of **essere** to give the idea of obligation ('must be', 'has to be', etc.):

La pizza **va fatta** in un forno molto caldo.	*Pizza has to be cooked in a very hot oven.*

The past participle agrees after **andare** and **venire** in the same way as after **essere**.

▼ Activity 7   *The passive*

Put the following active sentences into the passive:

a Il presidente inizia la discussione.
b Il cameriere ha portato altri bicchieri per lo spumante.
c Questa pioggia ha rovinato le mie scarpe.
d Quella povera ragazza ha rotto i piatti.
e Giulio ha pagato il conto.

■ Passive use of 'si'

It is very common to use **si** with the third person of the verb (singular or plural) instead of the passive construction. It cannot be used, however, when there is a phrase starting 'by' (**da**) – i.e. when there is an 'agent' of the passive. It is also normally used for things rather than persons:

Si vendono molte cose belle in questo negozio.	*A lot of lovely things are sold in this shop.*
L'arrosto **si serve** con pisellini e patate.	*The roast is served with peas and potatoes.*

It is really a construction with a reflexive verb, so when used in the perfect tense it takes **essere** and has the usual agreements:

Si è visto uno spettacolo straordinario.	*An extraordinary spectacle was seen.*
Non **si è potuto** andare.	*It was not possible to go.*

➤

In notices and small ads, you often find the **si** tacked on to the verb:

Aff<u>i</u>ttansi appartamenti (= si aff<u>i</u>ttano) *flats to let*
v<u>e</u>ndesi frigor<u>i</u>fero (= si vende)   *refrigerator for sale*

The passive **si** is not always translated into English as a passive construction. Instead, it is treated in the same way as the impersonal pronoun **si** (see page 66):

Si c<u>o</u>mprano molte cose a buon   *You can buy lots of things at*
prezzo nei saldi.   *a good price in the sales.*

Note: **sentire** means 'to hear', 'to listen to' and 'to smell'. When it is used with the reflexive pronoun (**mi sento, ti senti**, etc.) it means 'to feel'. When it is used with **si**, it has an impersonal or passive meaning:

Si sente fischiare il vento.   *You (can) hear the wind*
                                whistling.
Abbiamo sentito un bel concerto.   *We listened to (heard) a*
                                lovely concert.

▼ The imperfect tense

The perfect tense is used for an action that happened on one occasion and is finished. But there are times when we want to say that something 'used to happen', or 'was happening' – in other words, when we cannot put a precise end to what happened, so that the past we are describing is 'imperfect'. That is when we use the imperfect tense.

In English we say 'used to' or 'would' (as in 'every day he would go to the office') to talk about repeated actions in the past. And we use a past continuous ('was happening') to talk about an action that has no identified beginning or end.

In Italian, one tense does both of these jobs – the imperfect tense. It is very simple and, with the single exception of **<u>e</u>ssere**, all verbs are regular.

▼ Forming the imperfect tense

To form the imperfect, you add the following endings to the stem of the verb. For most verbs, the stem is the infinitive minus the '-re' ending, but see page 83 for verbs such as **fare**, **dire**, **condurre**, etc.

io	-vo
tu	-vi
lui	
lei }	-va
Lei	
noi	-vamo
voi	-vate
loro	-vano

comprare	vendere	dormire
compravo	vendevo	dormivo
compravi	vendevi	dormivi
comprava	vendeva	dormiva
compravamo	vendevamo	dormivamo
compravate	vendevate	dormivate
compravano	vendevano	dormivano

The only exception is **essere**:

ero
eri
era
eravamo
eravate
erano

▼ Activity 8   *The imperfect*

Write out the full imperfect tense of the following:

a finire
b portare
c volere
d chiedere
e andare
f fare
g sapere
h salire
i venire
j prendere
k chiudere
l dire

▼ *Using the imperfect tense*

As we have seen the imperfect tense is used:

- for a repeated or habitual action or event ('used to go', 'would go', 'went'):

Ogni giorno **andava** al mercato dove si **vendeva** la frutta.	*Every day he went (used to go) to the market where they sold fruit.*

- for an action or event without a definite beginning or end ('was going'):

Mentre **camminava guardava** la gente che **correva**.	*While he walked (was walking) he watched (would watch) the people rushing.*

- to describe things:

Faceva bel tempo e la piazza del mercato **era** piena di bancarelle.	*It was lovely weather and the market square was full of market stalls.*

You can also create a continuous past by using the imperfect of **stare** (**stavo**, etc.) + present participle:

come stavo dicendo	*as I was saying*

With the preposition **da** to describe something which started further back in time and was still going on in the past (see also page 95).

Lavorava in quella fabbrica da quindici anni.	*He had worked in that factory for fifteen years.*
Non pioveva da maggio.	*It had not rained since May.*

▼ Activity 9 *The imperfect*

Put the words in brackets into the imperfect tense. (The subject is given where it might be unclear.)

a Quando (io essere) in vacanza (leggere) moltissimo.
b (io preferire) i gialli* perchè non (loro essere) pesanti e non (io dovere) concentrarmi troppo.
c (io andare) ogni giorno alla spiaggia dove (io incontrare) gli amici. Ci (piacere) fare due chiacchiere (= *to have a chat*).

*'Un giallo' is the common expression for a thriller or detective story, because of an old and famous paperback series which had a standard yellow cover, 'i gialli Mondadori'.

▼ Perfect or imperfect?

The perfect tense tells us what happened; the imperfect tense gives us the background:

Ho visto un incidente ieri sera mentre **tornavo** a casa.	*I saw an accident yesterday evening while I was going back home.*
Parlavamo insieme quando, d'un tratto, **ha squillato** il telefono.	*We were talking together when, all of a sudden, the telephone rang.*
Sentivo un odore di gas e **mi sono sentito** male.	*I smelt a smell of gas and I felt ill.*

▼ Activity 10 *Perfect and imperfect tenses*

Replace the infinitive in brackets with the appropriate perfect or imperfect tense. (The subject is given where it might be unclear.)

a (io attraversare) la strada quando (vedere) il mio amico.
b (voi andare) alla Scala quando (essere) a Milano?
c Dove (tu essere) quando (io arrivare)?
d (tu conoscere) quel signore che ci (parlare)?
e (io cercare) un paio di scarpe rosse, ma invece ne (comprare) un paio di nere.

▼ The pluperfect tense

The perfect tense translates the English 'I have done', etc. When we go one step further back into the past, we say 'I had done', etc. – we use the past tense of 'to have' ('had') instead of the present ('have'). To do the same in Italian, you use the imperfect of **avere** or **essere** + past participle. This is known as the pluperfect tense:

Avevo già finito di mangiare quando sono entrati loro.	*I had already finished eating when they came in.*
Lui **era arrivato** prima di me.	*He had arrived before me.*

For the pluperfect of a passive verb, use the pluperfect of **essere** + past participle:

Il giorno prima **eravamo stati invitati** al ricevimento.	*We had been invited to the reception the day before.*

■ The perfect infinitive

The perfect infinitive of a verb is formed from the infinitive of **avere** or **essere** + the past participle of the verb.

Dopo esser stato a Milano, era andato a Roma.	*After having been in Milan, he had gone to Rome.*
Aveva visto tutto senza **aver aperto** gli occhi.	*He had seen everything without having opened his eyes.*
Eravamo contenti, pensando di **aver fatto** un buon lavoro.	*We were content, thinking we had done a good job.*

This construction can only be used when the subject of both parts of the sentence is the same.

▼ Activity 11 *The pluperfect*

Translate into Italian using the appropriate tenses:

a When we arrived he had already left.
b I had told you that I couldn't come.
c The car had stopped at the traffic lights.
d I thought she had bought the whole shop.
e I didn't know that you had already begun.

▼ The past definite tense (passato remoto)

The past definite tense is rapidly falling out of use in spoken Italian. It is never used in the North or in the standard Italian spoken on the radio and television, or in everyday written language. Instead, the perfect tense is normally used. The past definite is, however, still used in the spoken language in parts of southern Italy, and it is used widely in some types of journalism and in literature. Like the perfect tense, the past definite basically expresses a single action set in the past ('I bought'; 'I sold'; 'I finished'). This past is usually at some distance from the present (hence the tense's name in Italian, **passato remoto**). It is important to recognise and understand it for the purpose of reading.

▼ *Forming the past definite tense – regular verbs*
The regular forms are:

comprare	vendere	finire
comprai	vendetti (vendei)	finii
comprasti	vendesti	finisti
comprò	vendette (vendè)	finì
comprammo	vendemmo	finimmo
compraste	vendeste	finiste
comprarono	vendettero (venderono)	finirono

Note the alternative forms in '-ere' verbs in the **io**, **lui** and **loro** persons. The '-etti' forms are the more common, except where the stem of the verb ends in 't', when the other form is used (e.g. **potere** – **potei**).

▼ *Forming the past definite tense – irregular verbs*
Irregular verbs in the past definite are irregular only in the **io**, **lui** and **loro** persons. All the other persons follow the pattern above. And for any given verb, those three persons follow the same pattern. So as long as you know the first person (**io**) form, you can work out the rest of the tense (see the Verb Tables on pages 148–154).

Here are the past definite tenses of common irregular verbs:

- **avere**

ebbi, avesti, ebbe, avemmo, aveste, ebbero

- **venire**

venni, venisti, venne, venimmo, veniste, vennero

- **fare**

feci, facesti, fece, facemmo, faceste, fecero

- **dire**

dissi, dicesti, disse, dicemmo, diceste, dissero

- **conoscere**

conobbi, conoscesti, conobbe, conoscemmo, conosceste, conobbero

- **scendere**

scesi, scendesti, scese, scendemmo, scendeste, scesero

- **apparire**

apparvi, apparisti, apparve, apparimmo, appariste, apparvero

(See also the Verb Tables, pages 148–154.)

▼ **Activity 12**   *The past definite*

Write out the full past definite tense of the following verbs from the parts given:

a mettere (misi)
b vedere (vidi)
c volere (volli)
d sapere (seppi)
e scrivere (scrissi)
f prendere (presi)

Common exceptions
There are three verbs which do not follow this pattern:

- **essere**

fui, fosti, fu, fummo, foste, furono

• **dare**

diedi (detti), desti, diede (dette), demmo, deste, diedero (dettero)

• **stare**

stetti, stesti, stette, stemmo, stette, stettero

The past definite of **essere** used with a past participle forms a passive referring to a specific action in the past:

L'America **fu scoperta** nel mille quattrocento novantadue.

America was discovered in 1492.

The past definite of **avere** and **essere** can be used as auxiliaries with a past participle to form an equivalent to the pluperfect (called the past anterior). It is useful to recognise it, but it is never used in the spoken language:

Quando **ebbe finito**, si mise il capotto.

When he had finished, he put on his overcoat.

▼ Activity 13   *Past tenses*

Translate the following passage into English.

Quando arrivarono all'aeroporto, videro una folla ammassata davanti all'ingresso.

«Cosa c'è?» chiese Alessandra.

«Deve essere uno sciopero,» rispose suo marito.

«Lo sapevi già, allora!» esclamò lei, esasperata, «e non avevi detto niente!»

«No, cara. Certo che non lo sapevo,» disse lui. «L'ho letto adesso sui titoli dei giornali. Non vedi anche tu?» Le indicò il giornale che teneva in mano.

«Cosa facciamo adesso? Torniamo all'albergo?»

«Sì, è meglio. Ma prima dobbiamo parlare con la compagnia aerea per regolare i biglietti, altrimenti perdiamo non solo il volo ma anche i soldi.» Alzò la mano e chiamò un taxi.

«Hai ragione. Ma almeno così si prolunga la vacanza di qualche giorno, non è vero?» Se ne andarono sorridendo.

▼ The future tense

We have seen how you can use the present tense to mean the future (page 95). A more deliberate way to talk about a future action is to use the future tense. In English, the future tense is made up of the auxiliary 'shall' or 'will' and the main verb ('I shall/will buy', etc.). In Italian, there is only one word for each person of the verb. It is very easy to recognise and very easy to form, as all types of verbs have the same endings.

▼ *Forming the future tense – regular verbs*

To form the future tense of regular verbs, remove the 'e' from the infinitive and add the following endings. For '-**are**' verbs, however, you will first need to change the identity vowel from 'a' to 'e'.

io	-ò	noi	-emo
tu	-ai	voi	-ete
lui } lei } Lei }	-à	loro	-anno

Here is the future tense of the regular verbs:

comprare	vendere	finire
comprerò	venderò	finirò
comprerai	venderai	finirai
comprerà	venderà	finirà
compreremo	venderemo	finiremo
comprerete	venderete	finirete
compreranno	venderanno	finiranno

Remember to change the spellings to keep the sound:

- Verbs with infinitives ending in '-**care**' and '-**gare**' need an 'h' before the 'e' in the future to keep the hard 'k' or 'g' sound:

cercare – **cercherò**   pagare – **pagherò**

- Verbs ending in '-**ciare**' or '-**giare**' drop the 'i; because it is no longer needed to keep the soft 'c' or 'g' sound:

cominciare – **comincerò**   mangiare – **mangerò**

▼ *Forming the future tense – irregular verbs*

Verbs that are irregular in the future tense fall into three main groups:

- Some verbs drop the second-last vowel of the infinitive as well as the final 'e' before the endings above:

andare – **andrò**	avere – **avrò**
cadere – **cadrò**	dovere – **dovrò**
potere – **potrò**	sapere – **saprò**
vedere – **vedrò**	vivere – **vivrò**

- Some verbs have a double 'r' before the ending. The consonant in the stem may drop out to produce this:

venire – **verrò**	tenere – **terrò**
volere – **vorrò**	rimanere – **rimarrò**
valere – **varrò**	morire – **morrò** (also **morirò**)
bere – **berrò**	

- Verbs with an infinitive ending in '-**rre**' just drop the final 'e':

condurre – **condurrò**	tradurre – **tradurrò**
porre – **porrò**	ridurre – **ridurrò**

But:

- **essere:** sarò, sarai, sarà, saremo, sarete, saranno

Note: fare (**farò**), dare (**darò**) and dire (**dirò**) are regular.

(See also the Verb Tables on pages 148–154.)

▼ Activity 14   *The future tense*

Write out the full future tense of the following verbs:

a parlare	**f** scegliere (to choose)
b iniziare	**g** dormire
c pregare (to pray, ask)	**h** salire
d mettere	**i** arrivare
e giocare (to play)	**j** venire

▼ Activity 15   *The future tense*

Change the verbs in the following sentences from present to future:

a Andiamo a parlare con il direttore.
b Ri<u>du</u>cono i prezzi domani.
c Compro questo per mia moglie.
d Cercate un appartamento in centro?
e Lui vuole sempre venire con noi.

▼ *The future perfect tense*

To say 'I shall have done', 'they will have gone', etc. (the future perfect tense), use the future of **avere** or <u>e</u>**ssere** + past participle:

Domani **saranno partiti** per Roma.	*Tomorrow they will have left for Rome.*
Stasera **avremo finito** tutto.	*Tonight we will have finished everything.*

▼ *Using the future and future perfect tenses*

Other cases in which the future and future perfect are used are not always quite the same as in English:

* After expressions of time (**quando** = 'when'; **appena** = 'as soon as'), Italian uses the future where English uses the present:

Quando arriveranno glielo diremo.	*When they arrive we'll tell them.*

and the future perfect where English uses the perfect:

Appena avremo finito, andremo al bar.	*As soon as we've finished we'll go to the bar.*

* The future or future perfect is used for saying that something is probable, but not definite:

L'**avranno** già venduto.	*They will have already sold it.*
Avrà almeno cinquant'anni, ma non li dimostra.	*She must be at least fifty, but she doesn't look it.*

* **Se** ('if') can be followed by either the present or the future:

Non sò se **viene**. Non sò se **verrà**.	*I don't know if he'll come.*

Note: there is no equivalent of the continuous future ('he will be going', etc.) – the future is used instead:

Domani **pioverà**.   *It will be raining tomorrow.*

▼ Activity 16   *Using the future and future perfect*

Replace the infinitives in brackets with the future or future perfect tense as appropriate.

a   Tutti (venire). Noi (vedere) molti amici.
b   Lei (conoscere) mio marito, immagino. Lo (incontrare) in qualche riunione.
c   Dove (andare) i ragazzi? (Loro dovere) essere qui tra poco.
d   Appena (tornare) a casa vi (scrivere).
e   Quando (noi arrivare) a Milano, (noi andare) a tutti i negozi di via Monte Napoleone.

▼ The conditional tense

In English, we form the conditional tense by using the auxiliary verb 'would' (and sometimes 'should' with the first person), e.g. 'he said he would go'. The conditional in Italian is used in a similar way.

▼ *Forming the conditional tense*
The conditional tense in Italian is formed very much like the future, by removing the 'e' from the infinitive and adding the endings below. Just as in the future, the '-**are**' verbs change their identity vowel from 'a' to 'e'.

io	-ei
tu	-esti
lui	
lei	-ebbe
Lei	
noi	-emmo
voi	-este
loro	-ebbero

comprare	vendere	finire
comprer**ei**	vender**ei**	finir**ei**
comprer**esti**	vender**esti**	finir**esti**
comprer**ebbe**	vender**ebbe**	finir**ebbe**
comprer**emmo**	vender**emmo**	finir**emmo**
comprer**este**	vender**este**	finir**este**
comprer**ebbero**	vender**ebbero**	finir**ebbero**

If you follow the pattern set for the future tense, there is no problem in forming the conditional tense of any verb. For example:

Infinitive	Future (1st pers. sing.)	Conditional (1st pers. sing.)
essere	sarò	sarei
avere	avrò	avrei
volere	vorrò	vorrei
cadere	cadrò	cadrei

▼ Activity 17   *The conditional tense*

Write out the full conditional tense of the following verbs:

a potere   f bere
b dare   g fare
c dire   h spiegare
d sapere   i dimenticare
e piacere   j produrre

▼ *The conditional perfect tense*

To say 'he would have done', 'they would have gone', etc. (the conditional perfect tense), use the conditional of **avere** or **essere** + past participle:

Avrebbe potuto farlo.   *He could have done it.*
Sarebbero andati.   *They would have gone.*

▼ *Using the conditional and conditional perfect tenses*
Here are some ways in which the conditional is used in Italian:

- to express 'the future in the past', i.e. when the main verb in the past is talking about something that was then in the future. This often occurs with verbs to do with saying, thinking, etc.:

Ha detto che lo **venderebbe** a metà prezzo.	*He said he would sell it at half price.*
Sapevo benissimo che **non sarebbe venuto**.	*I knew very well that he wouldn't come.*
Sarebbe stato meglio dirmelo prima.	*It would have been better to tell me sooner (beforehand).*

- to express uncertainty, especially when it is something that is being reported but the facts are not completely confirmed yet, or there is a legal implication:

Dicono che il governo **sarebbe caduto**.	*They say the government has fallen.*
Il ministro **avrebbe accettato** delle bustarelle.	*The minister (allegedly) took bribes.*

- to make a request or a statement more polite or less direct:

Mi **darebbe** una mano, per favore?	*Would you give me a hand, please?*
Non **saprei**.	*I don't know (I wouldn't know).*

■ **Conditional use of 'potere', 'dovere' and 'volere'**
These verbs are very often used in the conditional form in everyday Italian:

- **potere** is used for politeness:

Potrebbe farmi un favore, per cortesia?	*Would you do me a favour, please?*

and has the sense of 'might' or 'could':

Giocando fuori casa **potrebbero** perdere.	*Playing away from home they might (could) lose.*

➤

- **dovere** in the conditional means 'ought to':

Dovresti provarlo in un'altro colore.	*You should (ought to) try it in another colour.*
Avrei dovuto prenderlo in rosso.	*I should have (ought to have) had it in red.*

- **volere** in the conditional means 'should/would like' and is the usual polite form of ordering something in a shop etc.:

Vorrei un caffè macchiato, per cortesia.	*I should like an espresso with a spot of milk, please.*
Avrei voluto accompagnarti, ma non potevo.	*I should like to have come with you, but I couldn't.*

■ Other ways of saying 'I would like', etc.:

Apart from **vorrei** etc., there are several ways of saying 'I would like':

- using **piacere**:

Mi piacerebbe anche una brioche.	*I would also like a bun.*
Ti piacerebbe un po' più di zucchero?	*Would you like a little more sugar?*

- using the adverb **volentieri** meaning 'willingly', 'with pleasure' (note that the ending does not change):

Paolo **verrebbe volentieri**, ma non può.	*Paul would like to come, but he can't.*

Note: 'could' can be the past or the conditional: if you can substitute 'was able', it is the past tense; if you can substitute 'would be able' it is the conditional. Similarly, 'would' can be the past (imperfect) if you can substitute 'used to'.

▼ Activity 18 · *Using the conditional tense*

Translate the phrases in brackets using conditional tenses where appropriate.

a (Would you like to) andare al cinema? (I should like to) vedere quel nuovo film italiano.
b (I should like to come), ma veramente (I ought to) studiare per gli esami.
c (May I see) delle cinture in cuoio, per favore?
d Quella (would suit you) bene, ma (it would be) meglio in un'altro colore.
e (They ought to have) dircelo. (We would have understood).

▼▼▼

DOUBTS AND COMMANDS
subjunctives and imperatives

▼ The subjunctive

The tenses we have seen so far have been **indicative**, because
they indicate things that occur, have occurred, will occur and
so on. The subjunctive is another mood: it expresses the sense
that something may or may not happen (or have happened). In
general, the subjunctive expresses uncertainty. Within the
subjunctive mood there are two tenses – present and past.

In Italian, unlike English, the subjunctive, both present and
past, is a normal part of everyday speech. It is quite simple to
form and to remember. When we see the subjunctive in
English, we recognise it because it seems to use the wrong
form: 'if I were' instead of 'if I was', 'be he rich or poor'
instead of 'is he'. In Italian, too, the present subjunctive seems
to have the wrong endings (**io compri** instead of **io compro**;
io venda instead of **io vendo**; **io finisca** instead of **io finisco**),
while the imperfect subjunctive stands out because of the
double 's' in the endings.

▼ *Forming the present subjunctive – regular verbs*
To form the present subjunctive of all verbs, take the first
person singular (**io**) of the present indicative tense and change
the endings as below.

Here are the regular patterns for the present subjunctive:

	comprare	vendere	dormire	finire
io tu lui lei Lei	compri	venda	dorma	finisca
noi	compriamo	vendiamo	dormiamo	finiamo
voi	compriate	vendiate	dormiate	finiate
loro	comprino	vendano	dormano	finiscano

Note the following points:

- There are really only two groups. Group 2 and Groups 3a and 3b have the same endings, except for the 'isc' in Group 3b.

- The identity vowel of Group 1 (-**are**) verbs changes to 'i', and that of groups 2 and 3 (-**ere** and -**ire**) to 'a'. (Hence the sense of the 'wrong' endings.)

- There is only the one form for the whole of the singular in each group.

- The **noi** form is the same as in the present indicative tense.

- The **voi** form has the same stem as the **noi** form and always ends in '-**iate**' (note the inserted -i-).

- In the **loro** form, the stress always falls on the third-last syllable.

▼ *Forming the present subjunctive – irregular verbs*

To form the present subjunctive of all verbs – even if they are otherwise irregular – take the first person singular (**io**) of the present indicative and change the endings as above.

- **mangiare** (mangio)

mangi, mangiamo, mangiate, mangino

- **cercare** (cerco)

cerchi, cerchiamo, cerchiate, cerchino

- **venire** (vengo)

venga, veniamo, veniate, vengano

- **potere** (posso)

possa, possiamo, possiate, possano

- **dovere** (debbo)

debba, dobbiamo, dobbiate, debbano

- **volere** (voglio)

voglia, vogliamo, vogliate, vogliano

- **andare** (vado)

vada, andiamo, andiate, vadano

(note: uses the 'a' endings)

- **fare** (faccio)

faccia, facciamo, facciate, facciano

(like an '-**ere**' verb because of the original '**facere**' infinitive)

- **dire** (dico)

dica, diciamo, diciate, dicano

- **fuggire** (fuggo)

fugga, fuggiamo, fuggiate, fuggano

- **ridurre** (riduco)

riduca, riduciamo, riduciate, riducano

- **porre** (pongo)

ponga, poniamo, poniate, pongano

- **uscire** (esco)

esca, usciamo, usciate, escano

See notes on pages 2–7 on how spelling changes are needed to keep pronunciation hard or soft.

The only verbs which do not use the **io** form of the present indicative to make the present subjunctive are **avere**, **essere**, **dare**, **stare** and **sapere**. In fact, they use the stem of the **noi** form and then follow the same general pattern.

avere	essere	dare	stare	sapere
abbia	sia	dia	stia	sappia
abbiamo	siamo	diamo	stiamo	sappiamo
abbiate	siate	diate	stiate	sappiate
abbiano	siano	diano	stiano	sappiano

(See also the Verb Tables, pages 148–154.)

▼ Activity 1   *The present subjunctive*

Write out the full present subjunctive of the following verbs:

a parlare
b cominciare
c vedere

d tenere (tengo)
e suggerire (-isc-)
f tradurre

▼ *The perfect subjunctive*

To make the perfect subjunctive, use the present subjunctive of
essere or **avere** as auxiliaries + past participle:

abbia mangiato   **siate** arrivati
si **siano** alzati

▼ *The imperfect subjunctive*

The imperfect subjunctive takes the stem of the infinitive and
adds the endings shown below. As in the imperfect indicative,
each verb group uses its own identity vowel.

io	-ssi
tu	-ssi
lui	
lei	-sse
Lei	
noi	-ssimo
voi	-ste
loro	-ssero

Here are the regular patterns, which apply to **all** verbs, except three:

comprare	vendere	finire
comprassi	vendessi	finissi
comprassi	vendessi	finissi
comprasse	vendesse	finisse
comprassimo	vendessimo	finissimo
compraste	vendeste	finiste
comprassero	vendessero	finissero

Verbs such as **fare**, **dire**, **ridurre**, etc. follow the same pattern as in the imperfect indicative: **facessi**, **dicessi**, **riducessi**, etc. **Avere** is quite regular:

avessi, avessi, avesse, avessimo, aveste, avessero.

The three verbs which use a different stem are:

essere	dare	stare
fossi	dessi	stessi
fossi	dessi	stessi
fosse	desse	stesse
fossimo	dessimo	stessimo
foste	deste	steste
fossero	dessero	stessero

▼ *The pluperfect subjunctive*

Like the pluperfect indicative, the pluperfect subjunctive takes us one step further back in the past from the imperfect. It is formed by using the auxiliaries **essere** and **avere** + past participle:

avessi dormito   **fossimo** entrati
vi **foste** incontrati

▼ Activity 2   *The imperfect subjunctive*

Write out the full imperfect subjunctive of the following verbs:

a preparare   d bere
b pregare   e capire (-isc-)
c ridere   f porre

▼ Using the subjunctive

In most cases, the subjunctive is used in a part of a sentence (a clause) which depends on the main clause. Many of these dependent clauses are introduced by the word **che** (= 'that'). Subjunctives are also used after words or phrases which are known as **conjunctions**, because they join two parts of a sentence together. Conjunctions such as **quindi** (= 'therefore') usually point to a definite fact, so are followed by an indicative tense. But some conjunctions give a sense of uncertainty, so they are followed by a subjunctive tense.

▼ *Conjunctions which are followed by the subjunctive*

The subjunctive must be used after the following conjunctions:

- **benchè, sebbene, quantunque, anche se** = 'although'

Lo prendo, **benchè sia** caro.   *I'll take it, although it's expensive.*

- **affinchè, perchè** = 'so that', 'in order that'

Lascio un messaggio **affinchè**   *I'll leave a message so that he*
sappia che siamo usciti.   *knows we've gone out.*

Remember that **perchè** followed by an indicative tense means 'because' or 'why'.

- **purchè, a patto che, a condizione che** = 'as long as', provided that', on condition that', 'providing'

Vengo con te **purchè** non ti   *I'll come with you as long as you*
arrabbi.   *don't get angry.*

- **a meno che . . . non** = 'unless'

Non possiamo accettare **a meno**   *We cannot accept unless someone*
che qualcuno **non** ci **venga** a   *comes to collect us.*
prendere.

- **caso mai, nel caso che, qualora** = 'in case', 'supposing'

Caso mai lo **veda**, ti darò le sue   *In case you see him, I'll give you*
chiavi.   *his keys.*

- **prima che** = 'before'

Devo finire **prima che ritornino.**   *I have to finish before they come back.*

- **senza che** = 'without'

Siamo usciti **senza che** ci
vedesse nessuno.

*We went out without anyone
seeing us.*

Note: with the expressions **prima** and **senza**, you use the
subjunctive only when the subjects of the main clause and the
dependent clause are different people. When the subject of
both clauses is the same person, you use the infinitive.

Devo finire **prima di ritornare**.

*I have to finish before coming
back.*

Siamo usciti **senza aver visto**
nessuno.

*We went out without having seen
anyone.*

▼ Activity 3 *Subjunctives after conjunctions*

**Complete the following sentences by using subjunctives to replace
the infinitives in brackets.**

a Aspetto ancora, anche se (<u>e</u>ssere) già tardi.
b Andiamo via domani, a meno che non (arrivare) qualche not<u>i</u>zia.
c Vuole andar via senza che lo (sapere) nessuno.
d Voglio comprarmi quella collana in oro prima che (<u>e</u>ssere)
   venduta.
e Rimarremo in questo albergo a condizione che ci (cambiare:
   they) la c<u>a</u>mera.

▼ *Verbs and phrases which are followed by the subjunctive*

The subjunctive is normally used in dependent clauses (usually
beginning with **che**) after the following types of verbs or
phrases:

- After verbs of wishing, preferring, suggesting, etc. + **che**:

With verbs expressing a will or a wish etc. such as the
following, you must use the subjunctive when the subject of
the main and dependent clauses are different people.

volere = *to want*
suggerire = *to suggest*

desiderare = *to wish, desire*
preferire = *to prefer*

Voglio che tu venga con me.

I want you to come with me.

But:

You must use the infinitive when the subject of both clauses is the same person:

Voglio venire con te.	*I want to come with you.*
Vuoi venire con me?	*Do you want to come with me?*
Vorrei che mi **facesse** un favore.	*I would like you to do me a favour.*
Avrei suggerito che **andaste** prima a ritirare i biglietti.	*I would have suggested that you went first to pick up the tickets.*

- With verbs of permitting, forbidding, advising and ordering + **che**, such as the following:

consigliare = *to advise*	dire = *to tell*
impedire = *to prevent*	lasciare = *to let, allow*
permettere = *to permit*	proibire = *to prohibit*
ordinare = *to order*	vietare = *to forbid*

Non lasciate che **facciano** tanto chiasso quei bambini.	*Don't let those children make such a racket.*

But:

You can also use the infinitive instead of the subjunctive:

Ti consiglio **di** non **prendere** il pesce.	*I advise you not to have the fish.*
Mi dice **di tacere**.	*He tells me to keep quiet.*
Lasciate **passare** la signora.	*Let the lady pass.*

After verbs expressing states of mind such as belief, opinion, emotion (fear, joy, sorrow, surprise, etc.), doubt and denial + **che**:

Ho paura che questa presa non **vada** bene per il mio rasoio.	*I'm afraid this socket may not be right for my razor.*
Mi dispiace che Sofia non **sia venuta**.	*I'm sorry Sofia hasn't come.*
Siamo contenti che **abbiate potuto** accettare l'invito.	*We're glad that you could accept the invitation.*
Abbiamo dubitato che **fosse** un vero Rolex.	*We doubted that it was a real Rolex.*
Non è vero che io **abbia** mai detto una cosa simile.	*It's not true that I ever said such a thing.*
Pensavamo che **fosse** qui il negozio, ma invece no!	*We thought the shop was here – but it isn't!*

Mi sembra che **sia** dietro l'angolo. *I think it's round the corner.*
Sì, credo che tu **abbia** ragione. *Yes, I think you're right.*

Note: often you may hear the indicative instead of the subjunctive where there is certainty about something that has already happened, but the subjunctive is still more normal.

- After verbs of seeing, knowing, understanding, etc. when used in the negative, when the verb is usually followed by **come** (= 'how') or **se** (= 'if' 'whether'):

Non vedo come **abbia** potuto sapere. *I don't see how he could have known.*
Non sappiamo ancora se **sia** possibile. *We don't know yet if it's possible.*

- After the following impersonal expressions and phrases:

bisogna che = *it is necessary that*
è possibile che = *it is possible that*
è bene che = *it is good that*
è inutile che = *it is useless (to)*
(è) peccato che = *it is a pity that*

Peccato che **sia** già chiuso. *Pity it's already closed.*
È inutile che si **lamenti**. *It is useless for you to complain.*

Note: if the subject of the dependent clause is also impersonal, you can use the infinitive instead of the subjunctive:

è inutile lamentarsi *it is useless to complain*

- After indefinite pronouns, adverbs and adjectives (usually ending in '-unque'):

chiunque = *whoever* dovunque = *wherever*
comunque = *however* qualunque/qualsiasi = *whatever*

Un premio a chiunque riesca ad indovinare! *A prize to whoever manages to guess!*
Seguila dovunque **vada**. *Follow her wherever she goes.*

Note: **qualunque** and **qualsiasi** are adjectives and must be followed by a noun. If you want to say 'whatever' on its own, you must say **qualunque cosa** or **qualsiasi cosa**.

- After superlative adjectives + **che**:

Questa è la migliore <u>o</u>pera ch'io **abbia** mai sentito.	*This is the best opera I have ever heard.*

▼ *The sequence of tenses*

The tense that you use for the subjunctive depends on the tense of the verb in the main clause. Basically, there is a present sequence, which leads to the present subjunctive or the perfect subjunctive (which is formed using the present subjunctive of <u>e</u>ssere or avere + the past participle), and a past sequence, which leads to the imperfect subjunctive or the pluperfect subjunctive. It works as follows:

Present sequence	
Main clause tense	**Dependent clause tense**
present/future/present conditional	present/perfect subjunctive
devo/dovrò finire *I must finish*	prima che rit<u>o</u>rnino/s<u>i</u>ano ritornati *before they return*

There is little difference in the meaning of the sentences, whatever combination of tenses is used.

Past sequence	
Main clause tense	**Dependent clause tense**
imperfect/past definite/ pluperfect/conditional perfect	imperfect/pluperfect subjunctive
dovevo/dovetti finire *I had to finish*	prima che ritorn<u>a</u>ssero/f<u>o</u>ssero ritornati *before they came back*
avevo dovuto finire *I had had to finish*	prima che ritorn<u>a</u>ssero/f<u>o</u>ssero ritornati *before they came back*
avrei dovuto finire *I ought to have finished*	prima che ritorn<u>a</u>ssero/f<u>o</u>ssero ritornati *before they came back*

The perfect tense in the main clause is followed by the present subjunctive when the action has not yet taken place (present sequence):

Ho lasciato un messaggio adesso **perchè sappia** che siamo usciti.	*I have left a message just now so that he'll know we've gone out.*

The perfect tense is followed by the imperfect subjunctive when the action has probably already taken place (past sequence):

Ho lasciato un messaggio ieri **perchè sapesse** che eravamo usciti.

I left a message yesterday so that he would know that we had gone out.

The conditional in the main clause can also be followed by either the present or the imperfect subjunctive, according to whether there is a sense of the future or the past (except in sentences containing 'if': see box below). Sometimes there is no strong feeling either way, so you can use either subjunctive tense, although the imperfect is possibly the more common:

dovrei finire prima che rit**o**rnino/ritorn**a**ssero.

■ The past sequence in 'if' clauses

In a sentence with 'if' in it, the main verb is often in the conditional or conditional perfect ('I would go if . . .', 'I would have gone if . . .'). In this case, the dependent clause beginning with 'if' (**se**) is always in the imperfect (or pluperfect) subjunctive:

Lo **comprerei** se **avessi** abbastanza soldi.

I would buy it if I had enough money.

Non **sar**e**bbero andati** se l'**av**e**ssero saputo.**

They wouldn't have gone if they had known (about) it.

This applies only in a past sequence; in the present, you use the indicative tenses:

Se non **è** vero, **è** ben trovato.

If it's not true, it's well invented.

Se lei me lo **chiede**, le **dirò** la verità.

If she asks me, I'll tell her the truth.

▼ Activity 4 — *Using the subjunctive*

Complete the following sentences by translating the words in brackets into Italian, using the subjunctive.

a Questo è il tempo più brutto che (I have) mai incontrato in Italia.
b Se (I were) ricco, mi comprerei una Ferrari.
c Non è possibile che (he does) tutto quel lavoro da solo.
d Non so come (they can) permettersi una casa così grande.
e Non sapevo che (he was) sposato.

▼ Giving commands: the imperative

When we want to tell someone to do something, i.e. give a command, we use the imperative. In English, we use a single word when we are addressing someone directly in the second person ('you'), e.g. 'go!', 'listen!' But we use a phrase when we are telling each other to do something, e.g. 'let us (let's) go!', 'let's listen!'

In Italian, the direct command (imperative) is used in the **tu**, **noi** and **voi** forms. (The polite **Lei** form works slightly differently and is covered on page 137.) In each case it consists of a single word, which is the same as the present tense (indicative), except for the **tu** form of '-**are**' verbs, which ends in 'a' instead of 'i':

	comprare	v<u>e</u>ndere	dormire	finire
tu	compra	vendi	dormi	finisci
noi	compriamo	vendiamo	dormiamo	finiamo
voi	comprate	vendete	dormite	finite

Verbs which have irregularities in the present tense follow the same pattern:

• **venire**

vieni, veniamo, venite

• **uscire**

esci, usciamo, uscite

The following is a list of the few verbs for which the imperatives differ from the present tense in some of their forms:

- **andare**

va, andiamo, andate

- **stare**

sta, stiamo, state

- **dire**

di', diciamo, dite

- **essere**

sii, siamo, siate

- **dare**

da', diamo, date

- **fare**

fa', facciamo, fate

- **avere**

abbi, abbiamo, abbiate

- **sapere**

sappi, sappiamo, sappiate

Note: **da'**, **di'** and **fa'** are usually written with an apostrophe, as are **va** and **sta**, but less so.

▼ *Object pronouns with the imperative*
The object pronouns (except **loro**) and the impersonal pronouns **ci** (**vi**) and **ne** come after the imperative and are joined on to it to form one word:

compratelo = *buy it*   finiscilo = *finish it*
prendiamone = *let's take some*   diteglielo = *say it to him*

Reflexive pronouns work in the same way:

<u>a</u>lzati = *get up*
ferm<u>a</u>tevi = *stop*
andi<u>a</u>mocene = *let's go (away)*

Loro also comes after the imperative but never joins on to it:

Insegna loro come farlo.   *Show them how to do it.*

The object pronoun doubles its initial letter when it joins up with va, da', sta, fa', and di' (and the apostrophe is dropped):

dammi = *give me*   d<u>a</u>mmelo = *give it to me*
fallo s<u>u</u>bito = *do it right away*   vattene = *go away*
Dicci come va il nuovo lavoro.   *Tell us how the new job's going.*

Note: the stress remains in the same place after the pronouns are added.

▼ Commands in the negative
To form a negative command, you put **non** in front of the **noi** and **voi** forms:

Non andate.   *Don't go.*
Non diciamo niente.   *Let's not say anything.*

Note: Italian always uses a double negative, i.e. 'let's not say nothing'.

But:
When you make the **tu** form negative, it changes to the infinitive, with **non** in front of it:

va! = *go!*   non andare! = *don't go!*
non fumare = *don't smoke*   non aspettare = *don't wait*

With the negative imperative, pronouns can either join up with the verb or come before it as separate words:

non and<u>a</u>rtene   }
non te ne andare   }   *don't go away*
non dici<u>a</u>molo a nessuno }
non lo diciamo a nessuno }   *let's not tell (it to) anyone*

■ **General instructions**

The infinitive is frequently used for instructions in public notices. The famous example, which used to be displayed in trains, was:

Non **sputare** nella carozza!   *No spitting in the compartment!*

It also appears in instructions such as recipes:

Portare a ebollizione il brodo.   *Bring the broth (stock) to the boil.*

▼ **Activity 5**   *Instructions*

Try to translate the following recipe into English. Perhaps you could also try to cook it. Some of the vocabulary is given below to help you.

Tagliatelle alle zucchine

Preparazione: 10 minuti - Cottura: 20 minuti

Ingredienti:
350g di tagliatelle fresche, 2 zucchine, 100g di cipolla, 25g di burro, 25g di farina bianca, 1 cucchiaino di curry piccante, 1 limone, prezzemolo, timo, un gambo di sedano, noce moscata, 1 bicchiere di brodo, sale

Pelate, lavate e tagliate a rondelle sottili la cipolla; pulite e lavate il prezzemolo, il sedano, il timo e tritateli finemente; pulite, lavate e tagliate le zucchine a listarelle sottili, nel senso della lunghezza.
Fate imbiondire in una casseruola la cipolla con il burro, poi unitevi le zucchine a listarelle e lasciatele insaporire alcuni secondi.
Aggiungete il trito di sedano, prezzemolo e timo, cospargete con la noce moscata grattugiata e con la farina e mescolate delicatamente. Unite il curry piccante, mescolate e bagnate con il brodo. Unite un poco di succo di limone e salate. Fate cuocere a fuoco basso la salsa per venti minuti. Nel frattempo fate cuocere le tagliatelle in abbondante acqua salata, scodatele bene e conditele con la salsa di zucchine. Versate in un piatto di portata e servite in tavola le tagliatelle calde.

➤

la cottura = *cooking (time)*	listarelle = *strips*
le zucchine = *courgettes*	imbiondire = *to fry till transparent*
cipolla = *onion*	insaporire = *to absorb the*
burro = *butter*	*flavour*
farina = *flour*	aggiungere = *to add*
un cucchiaino = *a teaspoon(ful)*	il trito (di sedano) = *the*
piccante = *hot (spicy)*	*chopped (celery)*
prezzemolo = *parsley*	cospargere = *to sprinkle*
timo = *thyme*	grattugiare = *to grate*
un gambo di sedano = *a stalk*	mescolare = *to stir*
of celery	bagnare = *to soak, wet*
noce moscata = *nutmeg*	il succo = *juice*
brodo = *broth (stock)*	cuocere = *to cook*
pelare = *to peel*	scolare = *to strain*
tagliare = *to cut*	condire = *to dress* (as in a salad)
rondelle = *rounds, rings*	versare = *to pour*
sottile = *thin*	un piatto di portata = *a serving*
pulire = *to clean*	*dish*
tritare = *to chop, mince*	

▼ *The imperative in the polite third person*

Commands given in the polite 'you' form (**Lei**) use the singular of the present subjunctive:

Venga domani . . . L'aspettaremo.	*Come tomorrow . . . we shall expect you.*
Prenda il numero cinque e **scenda** alla stazione centrale.	*Take the number five and get off at the central station.*

Object pronouns come before the verb:

Mi dia mezzo chilo di ciliege, per cortesia.	*Give me half a kilo of cherries, please.*
Ci chiami domani.	*Call us tomorrow.*
Si metta l'impermeabile, signora, sta piovendo.	*Put on your raincoat, (madam), it's raining.*
Non **me lo dica!**	*Don't tell me!*

but **loro** always follows the verb:

Dica loro di venire.	*Tell them to come.*

The present subjunctive is also used to give commands or to express wishes in the third person in a general sense, as in the English 'let', or 'may'. In this case it often (but not always) has **che** at the beginning of the phrase:

Nessun dorma.	*Let no-one sleep.*
(Che) lo facciano loro!	*Let them do it!*
Dio vi benedica.	*May God bless you.*
Viva l'Italia!	*Long live Italy!*

▼ **Activity 6**   *The polite imperative*

Translate these sentences into Italian using the polite imperative (the present subjunctive). The infinitives are given in brackets.

a Take a seat, sir. (accommodarsi)
b Be calm. (stare tranquillo)
c Have patience. (avere pazienza)
d Listen to me. (sentire or ascoltare)
e Go ahead. (andare avanti)

NUMBERS

▼ Cardinal numbers

0 = zero	11 = undici	21 = ventuno	31 = trentuno
1 = uno	12 = dodici	22 = ventidue	32 = trentadue
2 = due	13 = tredici	23 = ventitrè	33 = trentatrè
3 = tre	14 = quattordici	24 = ventiquattro	34 = trentaquattro
4 = quattro	15 = quindici	25 = venticinque	35 = trentacinque
5 = cinque	16 = sedici	26 = ventisei	36 = trentasei
6 = sei	17 = diciassette	27 = ventisette	37 = trentasette
7 = sette	18 = diciotto	28 = ventotto	38 = trentotto
8 = otto	19 = diciannove	29 = ventinove	39 = trentanove
9 = nove	20 = venti	30 = trenta	
10 = dieci			

40 = quaranta	70 = settanta
41 = quarantuno	71 = settantuno
45 = quarantacinque	80 = ottanta
50 = cinquanta	81 = ottantuno
51 = cinquantuno	90 = novanta
60 = sessanta	91 = novantuno
61 = sessantuno	etc.

100 = cento	500 = cinquecento
101 = centuno (centouno)	600 = seicento
102 = centodue (etc.)	700 = settecento
200 = duecento	800 = ottocento
300 = trecento	900 = novecento
400 = quattrocento	

1,000 = mille	1,000,000 = un milione
1,001 = mille e uno	2,000,000 = due milioni
1,980 = millenovecentottanta	1,000,000,000 = un miliardo
2,000 = duemila	2,000,000,000 = due miliardi
3,000 = tremila	

Cardinal numbers, except **milione** and **miliardo**, are adjectives. They are normally placed before the noun. Cardinal numbers are invariable in form, except for **uno** (**un, un', una**) and **mille** (plural: **mila**).

▼ Ordinal numbers

1st = primo	17th = diciasettesimo
2nd = secondo	18th = diciottesimo
3rd = terzo	19th = diciannovesimo
4th = quarto	20th = ventesimo
5th = quinto	21st = ventunesimo
6th = sesto	22nd = ventiduesimo
7th = settimo	30th = trentesimo
8th = ottavo	40th = quarantesimo
9th = nono	50th = cinquantesimo
10th = decimo	60th = sessantesimo
11th = undicesimo	70th = settantesimo
12th = dodicesimo	80th = ottantesimo
13th = tredicesimo	90th = novantesimo
14th = quattordicesimo	100th = centesimo
15th = quindicesimo	500th = cinquecentesimo
16th = sedicesimo	1,000th = millesimo

From 'eleventh' on, the ordinal number is formed by dropping the final vowel of the cardinal number and adding '-**esimo**' or '-**esima**'. If the cardinal number ends in 'è', it loses its accent but keeps the final vowel:

trentatrè = *thirty-three*   trentatreesimo = *thirty-third*

Ordinal numbers are adjectives and agree in gender and number with the nouns they refer to. They usually come before the noun, but follow the names of popes and kings or articles of the law:

il quarto posto   *the fourth seat*
la quinta fila   *the fifth row*
Giovanni Paolo secondo   *John Paul the second*
Carlo quinto   *Charles the fifth*
l'articolo quarto della costituzione   *article 4 of the constitution*

Ordinal numbers can be abbreviated by using a figure and adding º or ª:

la 5ª pagina   *the fifth page*
il 7º giorno   *the seventh day*

When referring to kings and popes, the following alternatives for 'eleventh' to 'nineteenth' are common:

11th = decimoprimo
12th = decimosecondo
13th = decimoterzo
14th = decimoquarto
15th = decimoquinto

16th = decimosesto
17th = decimosettimo
18th = decimottavo
19th = decimonono

Note: ordinals are always written as one word:

il quarantanovesimo giorno
il centocinquantesimo anniversario

the forty-ninth day
the hundred and fiftieth anniversary

▼ Fractions

Fractions are expressed as follows:

½ = mezzo, metà
⅓ = un terzo
⅔ = due terzi
¼ = un quarto
¾ = tre quarti
⅘ = quattro noni

$\frac{1}{10}$ = un decimo
$\frac{1}{11}$ = un undicesimo
$\frac{1}{20}$ = un ventesimo
$\frac{1}{100}$ = un centesimo
$\frac{1}{1000}$ = un millesimo
% = per cento

If **mezzo** is used as an adjective, it agrees with the noun to which it refers and is placed before it, usually without an article:

mezza giornata di lavoro
mezzo chilo di pane

half a day of work
half a kilo of bread

Mezzo is used as a noun in measurements and expressions of time, when it follows the noun to which it refers. It does not change its form (except sometimes in expressions of time):

Ho comprato due chili e mezzo di patate.
Sono le tre e mezzo/mezza.

I bought two and a half kilos of potatoes.
It is half past three.

The noun meaning 'half' in all other cases is (**la**) **metà**.

Ho preso soltanto metà della torta.
La metà di dodici è sei.
Verrò a metà settimana.
C'incontreremo a metà strada.

I only took half the cake.
Half of twelve is six.
I will come midweek.
We shall meet halfway.

▼ Odd and even

dispari = *odd*
pari = *equal*

per cinque = *in fives*
per dieci = *in tens*

I numeri dispari sono 1, 3, 5, etc.
Contare per cinque da 5 a 100.

The odd numbers are 1, 3, 5, etc.
Count in fives from 5 to 100.

▼ Collective numbers

un paio = *two, a pair of, a couple* (plural: paia)
una diecina = *about ten*
una dozzina = *a dozen, about twelve*
una quindicina = *about fifteen* (also = a fortnight)
una ventina = *about twenty*
un centinaio (plural: centinaia) = *about 100*
un migliaio (plural: migliaia) = *about 1,000*

The above collective numbers are all followed by **di**:

Ci saranno stati una trentina di
feriti.
C'erano migliaia di turisti a Roma.

There must have been about
thirty wounded.
There were thousands of tourists
in Rome.

The above collective numbers are often used to express age:

Lisa è sulla trentina.
Luca si avvicina alla quarantina.
Carlo ha superato la cinquantina.

Lisa is about thirty.
Luca is about forty.
Carlo has passed fifty.

▼▼▼ DATES AND TIME

▼ Days of the week

lunedì = *Monday*
martedì = *Tuesday*
mercoledì = *Wednesday*
giovedì = *Thursday*
venerdì = *Friday*
sabato = *Saturday*
domenica = *Sunday*

- Except for **domenica**, the days are masculine. They are not written with a capital letter.

- **Domenica** and **sabato** change for the plural, the others do not:

tutte le domeniche, tutti i sabati, tutti i giovedì

- To say 'on Tuesday', etc., simply say '**martedì**':

Martedì andiamo a Parigi.   *On Tuesday we're going to Paris.*

but use the definite article to indicate 'every':

il sabato, usciamo sempre con   *Every Saturday/On Saturdays we*
i bambini.   *always go out with the children.*

or use **tutti i sabati** or **ogni sabato**.

▼ Months of the year

gennaio = *January*
febbraio = *February*
marzo = *March*
aprile = *April*
maggio = *May*
giugno = *June*

luglio = *July*
agosto = *August*
settembre = *September*
ottobre = *October*
novembre = *November*
dicembre = *December*

- The months are masculine and are not written with a capital letter.

- To express 'in' with months, use either **a** or **in**:

Sono nato a/in maggio.   *I was born in May.*
A/In luglio fa caldo.   *It is warm in July.*

- Note also how to say 'on' a certain date:

il primo gennaio   *on the first of January*
il due febbraio   *on the second of February*

i.e. don't try to translate 'on' or 'of', and use the cardinal number except for **primo**.

- Note the following forms for asking and answering questions about the day of the month:

Che data è oggi?
Qual è la data di oggi?
Quanti ne abbiamo oggi?   *What is the date today?*
Oggi è il primo giugno.   *Today is the first of June.*
Oggi ne abbiamo tre.   *Today is the third.*

▼ Seasons of the year

la primavera = *spring*   l'autunno = *autumn*
l'estate (f.) = *summer*   l'inverno = *winter*

The names of the seasons are not written with an initial capital. They generally take the definite article:

Mi piace l'estate, ma preferisco   *I like summer, but I prefer*
l'autunno.   *autumn.*

But:
To indicate 'in' with seasons, either **in** or **di** (**d'**) without the definite article is used:

In inverno/D'inverno, vado a sciare.   *In winter I go skiing.*

▼ Years

millenovecentonovantas<u>ei</u> = *1996*

Alternatively, when written, it can be split up:

millenovecento novantas<u>ei</u>

The century can be said in several different ways:

il s<u>e</u>colo venti   *the twentieth century*
il vent<u>e</u>simo s<u>e</u>colo

But:
In Italian it is common to use **il Novecento** (= 'the 1900s'),
etc.:

il Quattrocento   *the fifteenth century (the 1400s)*
il Seicento   *the seventeenth century (the*
                         1600s)

▼ Time

il secondo = *second*   la sera, la serata = *evening*
il minuto = *minute*   la notte, la nottata = *night*
l'ora = *hour*   il giorno, la giornata = *day*
la mezz'ora = *half hour*   la settimana = *week*
la mattina ⎫   il mese = *month*
il mattino ⎬ = *the morning*   la stagione = *season*
la mattinata ⎭   l'anno, l'annata = *year*
il pomeriggio = *afternoon*   il s<u>e</u>colo = *century*

Note: **la mattina, la sera, la notte, il giorno** and **l'anno** are
used when talking about a precise unit of time. **La mattinata,
la serata, la nottata, la giornata** and **l'annata** indicate a more
vague sense of duration:

La dom<u>e</u>nica è il giorno di riposo.   *Sunday is the day of rest.*
Oggi è una bella giornata.   *Today is a beautiful day.*
Abbiamo passato un anno a Roma.   *We spent a year in Rome.*
Abbiamo avuto una buona annata.   *We had a good year.*
Questo vino è di una buona annata. *This wine is from a good year*
                                    (vintage).

Note the following phrases for telling the time of day in Italian:

Che ora è? ⎫	
Che ore sono? ⎭	*What time is it?*
È l'una.	*It is one o'clock.*
Sono le due (tre, etc.)	*It is two (three, etc.) o'clock.*
È mezzogiorno.	*It is noon.*
È mezzanotte.	*It is midnight.*
A che ora?	*At what time?*
Alle sei (precise, in punto).	*At six o'clock (sharp).*
Alle sette e cinque.	*At five past seven.*
Alle otto e un quarto.	*At quarter past eight.*
Alle nove e mezzo/mezza.	*At half past nine.*
Alle dieci meno un quarto.	*At quarter to ten.*
Alle ventuno e quarantacinque.	*At nine forty-five p.m.*
Alle undici meno dieci.	*At ten to eleven.*
Alle ventidue e cinquanta.	*At ten fifty p.m.*
Dalle due alle tre.	*From two till three.*
Sono le due e venticinque.	*It is twenty-five past two.*
Sono le otto meno venti.	*It is twenty to eight.*

The verb **mancare** can be used to express time before the hour:

Mancano venti minuti alle otto.	*It is twenty to eight.*

Time in the morning ('a.m.') is expressed by **del mattino** or **della mattina**:

Sono le nove del mattino.	*It is nine o'clock a.m.*

Time after noon ('p.m.') is expressed by **del pomeriggio, di sera (della sera)** or **di notte (della notte)**:

Sono le tre del pomeriggio.	*It is three in the afternoon (3.00 p.m.).*
Sono le otto di sera.	*It is eight in the evening (8.00 p.m.).*
Sono le undici di notte.	*It is eleven at night (11.00 p.m.).*

Note: the twenty-four-hour clock is used in Italy for timetables, and often for appointments:

alle tredici = *at 1.00 p.m. (13:00)*
alle sedici e venticinque = *at 4.25 p.m. (16:25)*
alle diciotto meno venti = *at 5.40 p.m. (17:40)*

▼▼▼
VERB TABLES

The following pages show some of the most commonly-used irregular verbs. These tables do not show the full form of every tense of the verb, and the following points should be borne in mind when using them:

- Only the irregular forms are given. Where the same pattern is followed in the whole tense, only the first person singular (**io**) is given.

- In the present indicative, the first person singular ending in '**-go**' is given where this is not obvious from the infinitive (e.g. **venire** – **vengo**). In these cases, the third person plural (**loro**) always follows the same form (**vengono**).

- The future tense is given in the first person singular only where it differs from the regular formation. The conditional follows the pattern of the future.

- The imperfect is always formed regularly from the stem, except in the verb **essere**, and so is not shown in the tables.

- The past definite (passato remoto) is always given in the first person singular. From this and the stem it is possible to form the whole tense.

- The past participle is shown only when it is irregular.

- The present subjunctive is given only where it is not formed from the present indicative. The imperfect subjunctive and imperative are not shown as they are regularly formed.

- Where a verb has alternative forms, these are given in brackets.

- There is more information in the chapters on Verbs (page 82) and Doubts and Commands (page 122).

• The following verbs have irregular forms in certain tenses:

Meaning	Infinitive	Present	Past definite	Past participle
switch on	**accendere**		accesi	acceso
also: apprendere, difendere, offendere, scendere, sospendere, comprendere, intendere, rendere, sorprendere, spendere				
notice	**accorgersi**		mi accorsi	accorto
also: porgere, sporgersi				
appear	**apparire**	appaio (apparisco)	apparvi (apparii)	apparso
also: comparire, scomparire				
open	**aprire**			aperto
also: coprire, scoprire, offrire, soffrire				
take on	**assumere**		assunsi	assunto
ask	**chiedere**		chiesi	chiesto
also: richiedere				
gather	**cogliere**	colgo	colsi	colto
also: accogliere, sciogliere, raccogliere, togliere				
lead	**condurre**	conduco	condussi	condotto
also: all verbs ending in -durre				
know	**conoscere**		conobbi	
also: riconoscere				
run	**correre**		corsi	corso
also: percorrere, soccorrere etc.				
decide	**decidere**		decisi	deciso
also: dividere, sorridere, ridere, uccidere				
say	**dire**	dico	dissi	detto
also: contraddire, benedire etc.				
direct	**dirigere**	dirigo	diressi	diretto
express	**esprimere**		espressi	espresso
extend	**estendere**		estensi	esteso
extract	**estrarre**	estraggo	estrassi	estratto
pretend	**fingere**		finsi	finto
lie down	**giacere**	giaccio	giacqui	

arrive at	**giungere**	giunsi	giunto
also: aggiungere, raggiungere			
read	**leggere**	lessi	letto
also: proteggere, eleggere			
put	**mettere**	misi	messo
also: ammettere, permettere, promettere etc.			
move	**muovere**	mossi	mosso
also: scuotere			
be born	**nascere**	naqui	nato
hide	**nascondere**	nascosi	nascosto
also: rispondere			
persuade	**persuadere**	persuasi	persuaso
also: evadere, invadere			
cry	**piangere**	piansi	pianto
break	**rompere**	ruppi	rotto
climb	**salire**	salgo	

choose	**scegliere**	scelgo	scelsi	scelto
write	**scrivere**		scrissi	scritto
also: descrivere, friggere (fritto), iscrivere, sconfiggere (sconfitto)				
turn off *extinguish*	**spegnere**	spengo	spensi	spento
squeeze	**stringere**		strinsi	stretto
also: costringere, restringere etc.				
win	**vincere**		vinsi	vinto

• The following verbs have future tenses formed irregularly:

Meaning	Infinitive	Present	Future	Past definite	Past participle
drink	**bere**		berrò	bevetti (bevvi)	bevuto
fall	**cadere**		cadrò	caddi	
put	**porre**	pongo	porrò	posi	posto
also: imporre, comporre, esporre etc.					

remain	**rimanere**	rimango	rimarrò	rimasi	rimasto
be worth	**valere**	valgo	varrò	valsi	valso
see	**vedere**		vedrò	vidi	visto (veduto)
live	**vivere**		vivrò	vissi	vissuto

- The following very common verbs have a number of tenses formed irregularly:

ANDARE to go

Present	**Indicative**	**Subjunctive**
	vado *I go*	vada *I go*
	vai	vada
	va	vada
	andiamo	andiamo
	andate	andiate
	vanno	vadano
Future	andrò *I shall go*	

DARE to give

Present	**Indicative**	**Subjunctive**
	do *I give*	dia *I give*
	dai	
	da	
	diamo	
	date	
	danno	
Future	darò *I shall give*	
Past definite	diedi (detti) *I gave*	
	diesti	
	diede (dette)	
	demmo	
	deste	
	diedero (dettero)	
Imperfect subjunctive	dessi *I gave*	

DOVERE to have to, must

Present	**Indicative**	**Subjunctive**
	devo (debbo) *I must*	debba *I must*
	devi	
	deve	
	dobbiamo	

dovete
d<u>e</u>vono (debbono)

| *Future* | dovrò *I shall have to* |

FARE *to do, make*

Present indicative	faccio *I make*
	fai
	fa
	facciamo
	fate
	fanno

Future	farò *I shall make*
Past definite	feci *I made*
Past participle	fatto *made*

MORIRE *to die*

Present	**Indicative**	**Subjunctive**
	muoio *I die*	muoia *I die*
	muori	
	muore	
	moriamo	
	morite	
	mu<u>o</u>iono	

| *Future* | morirò (morrò) *I shall die* |
| *Past participle* | morto *dead* |

PARERE *to seem*

Present	**Indicative**	**Subjunctive**
	paio *I seem*	paia *I seem*
	pari	
	pare	
	pariamo	
	parete	
	p<u>a</u>iono	

Future	parrò *I shall seem*
Past definite	parvi *I seemed*
Past participle	parso *seemed*

P<u>E</u>RDERE *to lose*

Past definite	persi (perdetti) *I lost*
	perdesti
	perse (perdette)
	perdemmo
	perdeste
	p<u>e</u>rsero (perd<u>e</u>ttero)

| *Past participle* | perso (perduto) *lost* |

PIACERE *to please*

Present	Indicative	Subjunctive
	piaccio *I please*	piaccia *I please*
	piaci	
	piace	
	piacciamo	
	piacete	
	piacciono	
Past definite	piacqui *I pleased*	
Past participle	piaciuto *pleased*	

POTERE *to be able*

Present indicative	
	posso *I am able*
	puoi
	può
	possiamo
	potete
	possono
Future	potrò *I shall be able*

SAPERE *to know*

Present	Indicative	Subjunctive
	so *I know*	sappia *I know*
	sai	
	sa	
	sappiamo	
	sapete	
	sanno	
Future	saprò *I shall know*	
Past definite	seppi *I knew*	

SEDERSI *to sit down*

Present	Indicative	Subjunctive
	mi siedo (seggo) *I sit down*	mi sieda (segga) *I sit down*
	ti siedi	
	si siede	
	ci sediamo	
	vi sedete	
	si siedono (seggono)	
Past definite	mi sedetti *I sat down*	
also **possedere**		

SPINGERE *to push*

Past definite	spinsi *I pushed*
	spingesti
	spinse
	spingemmo
	spingeste
	spinsero
Past participle	spinto *pushed*

also **distinguere, fingere, dipingere**

STARE *to be, stay*

Present	**Indicative**	**Subjunctive**
	sto *I am*	stia *I am*
	stai	
	sta	
	stiamo	
	state	
	stanno	
Future	starò *I shall be*	
Past definite	stetti *I was*	
	stesti	
	stette	
	stemmo	
	steste	
	stettero	
Imperfect subjunctive	stessi *I was*	

TENERE *to hold*

Present indicative	tengo *I hold*
	tieni
	tiene
	teniamo
	tenete
	tengono
Future	terrò *I shall hold*
Past definite	tenni *I held*

also **mantenere, ottenere, contenere**, etc.

TRARRE *to pull*

Present	**Indicative**	**Subjunctive**
	traggo *I pull*	tragga *I pull*
	trai	
	trae	
	traiamo	
	traete	
	traggono	

Imperfect	traevo *I was pulling*	traessi *I was pulling*
Past definite	trassi *I pulled*	
Past participle	tratto *pulled*	

also **attrarre, sottrarre**

USCIRE *to go out*

Present	**Indicative**	**Subjunctive**
	esco *I go out*	esca *I go out*
	esci	esca
	esce	esca
	usciamo	usciamo
	uscite	usciate
	escono	escano

also **riuscire**

VENIRE *to come*

Present indicative	vengo *I come*
	vieni
	viene
	veniamo
	venite
	vengono
Future	verrò *I shall come*
Past definite	venni *I came*
Past participle	venuto *came*

also **avvenire, pervenire** etc.

VOLERE *to want*

Present indicative	voglio *I want*
	vuoi
	vuole
	vogliamo
	volete
	vogliono
Future	vorrò *I shall want*
Past definite	volli *I wanted*

▼▼▼ ANSWERS TO ACTIVITIES

▼ *Articles and nouns*

Activity 1
a una donna
b gli u<u>o</u>mini
c uno studente
d la casa
e le sedie
f un ragazzo
g un'antenna
h i bambini
i gli studenti
j gli acquisti
k l'argento
l un uovo
m lo zio
n gli stivali
o Il signor Volante è professore.
p È un bravo professore.
q La ragazza è americana.
r È nella camera numero uno.
s Gli americani sono simp<u>a</u>tici.

Activity 2
a i giorni
b i letti
c gli zucchini
d gli <u>a</u>ngoli
e i conti
f gli sforzi
g i panini
h gli ingressi

Activity 3
a le signore
b le tazz<u>e</u>
c le olive
d le scarpe
e le forchette
f le saponette
g le <u>a</u>natre
h gli aromi

Activity 4
a le notti
b i fiori
c le lenti
d le unioni
e le croci
f i colori
g i giocatori
h gli or<u>e</u>fici

Activity 5
a un/il forno, i forni
b un/il fuoco, i fuochi
c una/la cucina, le cucine
d un/il bicchiere, i bicchieri
e una/la luce, le luci
f uno/lo sgabello, gli sgabelli
g un'/l'erba, le erbe
h un/il gas, i gas
i un/il dito, le dita
j una/la carne, le carni
k un/il guanto, i guanti
l una/la fiamma, le fiamme

m una/la pentola, le pentole   q un/l'odore, gli odori
n un/il peperone, i peperoni   r una/la mano, le mani
o un'/l'arancia, le arance   s un/l'uovo, le uova
p uno/lo straccio, gli stracci   t una/la bistecca, le bistecche

▼ *Adjectives*

Activity 1

a la Casa Bianca
b Il mondo è piccolo.
c La cravatta è rossa e nera.
d I miei genitori sono vecchi.
e Le ragazze sono giovani.
f La strada non è difficile, ma è lunga.

Activity 2

a La povera ragazza è innamorata.
b Roberto è un vecchio compagno di classe.
c Che bei fiori!
d Questo è un buon esempio del lavoro di un grande scultore.

Activity 3

a Dov'è la fermata più vicina?
b L'arrosto è eccellente, è tanto saporito, ma il vitello è migliore.
c Fa più caldo qui che a casa.
d Però non fa così caldo come l'anno scorso.
e Io mangio meno di mio marito.

Activity 4

a Le presento mia moglie, mio figlio e il suo amico Mario.
b Dove sono i nostri passaporti?
c Buona sera, signora. La Sua tavola è pronta.
d La loro casa è molto bella.
e Ecco la Sua valigia, signore.

Activity 5

a Quei pomodori sono troppo piccoli. Questi sono migliori.
b Non sono gli stessi? No, sono molto più grandi.
c Tutto è pronto? Andiamo tutti.

Activity 6
- Avete una camera grande, per caso?
- Certo, signorina, tutte le nostre camere sono grandi.
- È per i miei genitori.
- Per quanto tempo? Più di una settimana?
- No, meno. Tre giorni, se tutto va bene.

Activity 7
- Questo sembra un bel ristorante. C'è molta gente, la carta è buonissima, con piatti diversi.
- Sì, e costa poco.
- Io prendo le lasagne verdi. E tu?
- Io prendo lo stesso. Vuoi un po' di vino?
- Sì. Che vino è quello?
- È un nostro vino locale.
- È buono?
- È ottimo. I nostri vini sono tanto buoni quanto i vini francesi, spesso anche migliori.
- Allora, salute! E buon appetito!

Activity 8
a Ci sono degli errori sul conto. Abbiamo avuto del vino rosso, ma non abbiamo ordinato acqua minerale.
b Nella cattedrale ci sono delle belle cose. Alcuni quadri sono di Giotto.
c Voglio del pane e alcuni panini.
d Ho visto dei prezzi esagerati in qualche negozio.
e Non abbiamo nessuna intenzione di venire.

▼ Adverbs
Activity 1
a liberamente
b francamente
c onestamente
d facilmente
e semplicemente
f gratuitamente
g dolcemente
h probabilmente
i difficilmente
j teneramente

Activity 2
a Lei cucina in una maniera squisita/un modo squisito.
b Ci accoglie in una maniera/un modo amichevole.
c Parla in una maniera franca/in un modo franco/con franchezza.

d Dice la verità in una maniera aperta/in un modo aperto.
e Annuncia in una maniera/un modo autorevole/con autorità le ultime pettegolezze.

Activity 3

a Andiamo dentro perchè è già tardi.
b Andate direttamente alla stazione. Vi raggiungeremo il più presto possibile.
c Mi va bene la minigonna? Dimmi onestamente.
d Non so esattamente. Forse sarebbe meglio prenderla leggermente più lunga.
e Detto con molta delicatezza e diplomazia/in modo delicatissimo e diplomatico! Ma parla più piano!

▼ *Pronouns*

Activity 1

a 'Mi chiamano Mimi' è un'aria bellissima, e lei la canta bene.
b Ciao, Franco, ti telefono domani.
c Gli abbiamo già dato i soldi.
d Ma non ci ha dato una ricevuta.
e Non mi importa – la riceveremo domani.

Activity 2

a Il conto? Glielo pago domani.
b Prendo queste scarpe. Me le può tenere fino a stasera?
c L'Albergo Belvedere – ce lo può raccomandare?
d Cerco la via Cavour. Me la può indicare, per cortesia?
e Deve essere vero, se me lo dici tu.

Activity 3

a Prendo queste scarpe. Può tenermele fino a stasera?
b L'Albergo Belvedere – può raccomandarcelo?
c Cerco la via Cavour. Può indicarmela, per cortesia?

Activity 4

a Mi metto le scarpe.
b Si lava i capelli.
c Loro si vedono ogni giorno.
d Io vado a farmi un favore.

Activity 5
a Amo te, non lei. Vieni con me.
b Giocano per se stessi, non per la squadra.
c Gli spaghetti sono per me, le tagliatelle per loro.
d La vita è cara da voi.
e Puoi andare da solo, senza (di) me.

Activity 6
a Where does one pay?
b You have to go to the counter.
c Thanks. Can I pay with a credit card?
d Of course. Today credit cards are a fact of life.
e Yes – and we spend too much!

Activity 7
a Vuole giornali inglesi, ma non ce ne abbiamo.
b C'è un posto libero? No, non ce n'è.
c Vieni alla partita? Ci andiamo tutti.
d Lei conosce il dottor Loversi. Ne abbiamo parlato ieri.
e Ci sono gelati da duemila lire? Sì, quanto ne vuole?

Activity 8
– Andiamo a quel negozio nel quale abbiamo visto quelle
  belle borse ieri. Puoi comprarmene una?
– Ah, eccolo!
– No, non è questo negozio, è quello piccolo. Ci vado da
  sola; puoi fare quello che vuoi (tu), non mi importa.
– Vorrei la borsa nera che ho visto ieri – quella grande. La
  mia è vecchia, e troppo piccola. Da noi, non ce ne sono –
  non così belle come queste. La prendo.
– Gliela la metto in carta da regalo?
– No – il regalo è per me . . . ma paga lui!

▼ *Prepositions*
Activity 1
a Vieni con me dal parrucchiere. Il negozio è di fronte all'
  albergo.
b Questa è la strada che va verso Siena. Viene da Bologna e
  passa per Firenze.
c Andiamo in città. Prendiamo il tram fino alla piazza.
  Possiamo mangiare nella trattoria accanto al duomo.
d La mensa degli studenti è dietro l'angolo a destra.
e Cerco di finire, ma ho troppo da fare.

▼ *Verbs*

Activity 2

– Perchè non vuoi (vuole) venire domani? Non ti (Le) piace la campagna?
– Devo andare a comprare un regalo per mio marito. Conosci (conosce) un negozio dove vendono delle belle cravatte?
– Non so dove sono i negozi migliori.
– Possiamo chiedere nell'albergo. (Loro) sanno tutto.

Activity 3

a Non posso venire per il momento. Sto scrivendo una lettera a mia madre.
b (Che) cosa vuole quel signore (quell'uomo)? Ci sta chiamando.
c Dove va questo autobus? Io voglio andare a via Manzoni.
d Conosci (conosce, conoscete) bene Milano? Devo essere al mio albergo alle cinque.
e Mi piace viaggiare in autobus perchè posso vedere tutta la città.

Activity 4

a ho comprato
b abbiamo dormito
c hanno preso
d abbiamo voluto
e avete potuto
f hai venduto
g ho finito
h ho detto
i hanno saputo
j ha aperto

Activity 5

a Vedi quella signora? L'ho incontrata ieri.
b Le abbiamo dato i regali che abbiamo comprato.
c Non trovo più le chiavi. Penso che le ho perse.
d Vi abbiamo visto (visti) ieri sera al concerto.
e Buongiorno, signora Viggiani. L'ho chiamata per telefono ma non l'ho trovata a casa.

Activity 6

a La settimana scorsa siamo andati a vedere La Traviata alla Scala. Mi è piaciuta molto.
b Tutti e tre ci siamo incontrati davanti all'ingresso principale.
c Siamo entrati e siamo saliti alla prima galleria.
d L'opera è cominciata alle otto ed è finita a mezzanotte.
e Quando siamo usciti, siamo corsi (abbiamo corso) per prendere l'ultimo tram.

Activity 7
a La discussione è iniziata dal presidente.
b Altri bicchieri per lo spumante sono stati portati dal cameriere.
c Le mie scarpe sono state rovinate da questa pioggia.
d I piatti sono stati rotti da quella povera ragazza.
e Il conto è stato pagato da Giulio.

Activity 9
a Quando ero in vacanza leggevo moltissimo.
b Preferivo i gialli perchè non erano pesanti e non dovevo concentrarmi troppo.
c Andavo ogni giorno alla spiaggia dove incontravo gli amici. Ci piaceva fare due chiacchiere.

Activity 10
a Attraversavo (stavo attraversando) la strada quando ho visto il mio amico.
b Siete andati alla Scala quando eravate a Milano?
c Dove eri quando sono arrivato (-a)?
d Conoscevi quel signore che ci ha parlato?
e Cercavo un paio di scarpe rosse, ma invece ne ho comprato un paio di nere.

Activity 11
a Quando siamo arrivati, (lui) era già partito.
b Ti (le, vi) avevo detto che non potevo venire.
c La macchina si era fermata al semaforo.
d Pensavo (ho pensato) che aveva comprato tutto il negozio.
e Non sapevo che avevate (avevi, aveva) già cominciato.

Activity 13
When they arrived at the airport, they saw a crowd amassed in front of the entrance.
'What's up?' asked Alessandra.
'It must be a strike,' replied her husband.
'You knew it already, then!' she exclaimed in exasperation, 'and you hadn't said anything!'
'No, darling. Of course I didn't know,' he said. 'I read it just now in the newspaper headlines. Can't you see too?' He showed her the newspaper he was holding (in his hand).
'What do we do now? Shall we go back to the hotel?'
'Yes, it's best to. But first we have to speak to the airline to

sort out the tickets, or otherwise we'll lose not only the flight but the money as well.' He raised his hand and called a taxi. 'You're right. But at least this way we prolong our holiday by a few days, don't we?' They went away smiling.

Activity 15
a Andremo a parlare con il direttore.
b Ridurranno i prezzi domani.
c Comprerò questo per mia moglie.
d Cercherete un appartamento in centro?
e Lui vorrà sempre venire con noi.

Activity 16
a Tutti verranno. Noi vedremo molti amici.
b Lei conoscerà mio marito, immagino. Lo avrà incontrato in qualche riunione.
c Dove saranno andati i ragazzi? Dovranno essere qui tra poco.
d Appena saremo tornati a casa vi scriveremo.
e Quando arriveremo a Milano, andremo a tutti i negozi di via Monte Napoleone.

Activity 18
a Vorresti andare al cinema? Io vorrei/Mi piacerebbe vedere quel nuovo film italiano.
b Mi piacerebbe venire/Verrei volontieri, ma veramente dovrei studiare per gli esami.
c Potrei vedere delle cinture in cuoio, per favore?
d Quella ti/Le starebbe bene, ma sarebbe meglio in un'altro colore.
e Avrebbero dovuto dircelo. L'avremmo capito.

▼ *Doubts and commands*
Activity 3
a Aspetto ancora, anche se sia già tardi.
b Andiamo via domani, a meno che non arrivi qualche notizia.
c Vuole andar via senza che lo sappia nessuno.
d Voglio comprarmi quella collana in oro prima che sia venduta.
e Rimarremo in questo albergo a condizione che ci cambino la camera.

Activity 4
a Questo è il tempo più brutto che io abbia mai incontrato in Italia.
b Se fossi ricco, mi comprerei una Ferrari.
c Non è possibile che faccia tutto quel lavoro da solo.
d Non so come possano permettersi una casa così grande.
e Non sapevo che fosse sposato.

Activity 5
Preparation: 10 minutes – Cooking time: 20 minutes

Ingredients:

350g of fresh tagliatelle, 2 courgettes, 100g of onions, 25g of butter, 25g of white flour, 1 teaspoon of hot curry powder, 1 lemon, parsley, thyme, a stalk of celery, nutmeg, 1 glass of stock, salt

Peel, wash and cut the onion into thin rings; clean and wash the parsley, the celery and the thyme and chop them finely; clean, wash and chop the courgettes into thin strips lengthwise. Sauté the onion in a casserole with the butter until transparent, then add the strips of courgette and let them sauté for a few seconds. Add the chopped celery, parsley and thyme, sprinkle with the grated nutmeg and flour and gently stir. Add the hot curry powder, stir and pour in the stock. Add a little lemon juice and add salt. Cook the sauce on a low heat for twenty minutes. In the meantime boil the tagliatelle in plenty of salted water, strain it well and dress it with the courgette sauce. Pour the tagliatelle into a serving dish and serve hot.

Activity 6
a Si accomodi.
b Stia tranquillo.
c Abbia pazienza.
d Mi senta/Mi ascolti.
e Vada avanti.

▼▼▼
INDEX

A

a (ad)
- = by 73
- + definite article 73
- + emphatic pronoun 63
- + infinitive 78,80

a/an (indefinite article) 9–11
active verbs 104
adjectives
- absolute superlatives 30
- agreement of 23–5
- as adverbs 87
- comparison 29–32
- demonstrative 36
- indefinite (of quantity) 38, 42–3
- interrogative 40
- negative 43
- position of 25
- possessive 33–5
- short forms 26–7
- suffixed modifiers 28
- superlative 29–32

adverbs
- absolute superlatives 51
- adverbial phrases 46–7
- comparison 51–2
- formation of 45–6
- of place 49–50
- position of 50
- of quantity 48
- of time 48–9

alcuni/alcune 43
andare 92
any 42
articles
- definite 10–12
- indefinite 9–11

at 72–3
avere 90
- as auxiliary verb 99
- common expressions with 90–91

B

bello 27–8
better 52
buono 26

C

cattivo 31
c'è/ci sono 67
- negative 43–4, 67
che 69
- in questions 84
- + subjunctive 127–30
ciò 67
ciò che 70–71
commands
- form of 133–8
- negative 135
- position of pronouns 134–5
comparisons 29–32, 51–2
conditional 117
- formation of 117–18
- uses of 119
conditional perfect 118
- uses of 119
conoscere 93
consonants 4–7
cui 69–70

D

da 74
- + emphatic pronoun 64–5
- in expressions of time 95
- with passive verbs 104

dates 143–5
definite articles 10–12
di
- + definite article 72
- + emphatic pronoun 64
- + infinitive 79–80
dovere 94, 102–3, 119–20

E

ecco 61
essere 90
- as auxiliary verb 101–3

F

fare 92
- common expressions with 93
(a) few 38
from 74
future 114
- formation of 114–15
- uses of 114, 116–17
future perfect 116
- formation of 116
- uses of 116

G

gender 13–16
grande (gran) 26–7

H

have 90
have/get something done 92
his/hers 33–5

I

il/lo/la/i/gli/le 10–12
il quale/la quale/ i quali/le quali 70
imperatives
- formation of 133–8

negative 135
position of
    pronouns in 134–5
imperfect 106
formation of 107
uses of 106, 108–9
in 76
indefinite articles
    9–11
indefinite expressions
    130
indicative 123
indirect objects
    57–61
infinitives 82–3
    perfect 110
    prepositions +
        77–81
    sapere + 94

L
Lei 55–6
loro
    possessive 33–4
    object/emphatic
        pronoun
        57–9, 135

M
meglio 52
migliore 30
mio 33–4
mine 33–4

N
ne 68
nessuno 39, 43
nostro 33
nouns
    gender 13–16
    plurals 13–18
    suffixed modifiers
        21–2
    variable nouns 15
numbers 10, 139–42
    with **ne** 68
nuovo 25

O
occorrere 86
of 72, 74
ours 33

P
participles see past
    participles; present
    participles
passive of verbs
    formation of 104–6
    uses of 104–6
past definite111
    formation of 111–13
past participles 97–8
    agreement of 100–2
    formation of 98
PDO see preceding
    direct objects
per 76
perfect 97
    formation of 97–101
    uses of 97, 109
perfect subjunctive
    125
piacere 86, 120
pluperfect 110
    formation of 110
pluperfect subjunctive
    126
plurals 10–12
po': un po' di 38
potere 93, 102, 119
preceding direct
    objects 100–101
prepositions
    + definite article 72
    before infinitives
        78–81
    before nouns 72–3
    in combination
        64, 73, 75
present
    formation of 87–90
    uses of 87, 95
present conditional
    132
present participle 96
present subjunctive
    122–5
pronouns
    demonstrative
        36, 69
    direct object 56–61
    emphatic 63–5
    impersonal 66–7
    indefinite 130

indirect object
    56–61
    order of 57–61
    personal 54
    position of 58–60
    possessive 33–5, 68
    reciprocal 62
    reflexive 61–3
    relative 69–70
    subject 55–6

Q
quello che 70–1
questo/quello 36
questions 84

R
reflexive pronouns
    61–3
reflexive verbs 102
    = passive 105

S
same 37–8
santo 28
sapere 93–4
se 132
servire 86
should 120
some 42
stare
    in expressions of
        health 52, 96
    in present
        continuous 95–7
stare per 96
stesso 65
subjunctive 122
    formation of 122–6
    structures requiring
        127–32
suo 33–5
    di Lei 35

T
tenses; see names of
    individual tenses
that
the (definite article)
    10–12
theirs 33–4
them 57–9

this/that/these/those
36–7
   demonstrative
      pronoun 36
   relative pronoun
      69–70
time, expressions of
   145–7
to 72–3, 76
tu 55
tuo 33
tutto 39

U
un(o)/una 9–11

V
verbs
   agreement with
      subject 83
   conjugations 82–3
   impersonal 85
   irregular 148–54
   negative 85
   reflexive 61–2,
      105–6
voi 55
volere 94, 102–3,
   119–20
vostro 33
vowels 2–4

W
weather 93
what? 84
who/which/that/whose
   69–70

Y
you 55–6
yours 33–4